Kasha Nabagesera

Battling for LGBTQ Rights in Uganda – Unauthorized

Aria Oluwaseun

ISBN: 9781779695970
Imprint: Telephasic Workshop
Copyright © 2024 Aria Oluwaseun.
All Rights Reserved.

Contents

Introduction   1
The life and activism of Kasha Nabagesera   1

A Spark in the Darkness   11
The Awakening   11
Organizing for Change   21
Defiance and Determination   30

A Beacon of Hope   41
Building Bridges   41
The Battle Continues   49
Forging an International Movement   57

A Legacy of Change   65
The Impact of Kasha's Work   65
Personal Sacrifices and Triumphs   73

Conclusion   83
The ongoing struggle for LGBTQ rights in Uganda   83

Epilogue: Fighting for Equality   91
Kasha's Continued Activism   91

Index   99

Introduction

The life and activism of Kasha Nabagesera

Early years and upbringing

Kasha Nabagesera was born in a small town in Uganda, a country often characterized by its vibrant culture and rich traditions, but also by its stringent societal norms. Growing up in a conservative environment, Kasha's early years were marked by a blend of familial love and the looming shadow of societal expectations. Raised in a close-knit family, she was taught the values of respect, hard work, and community. However, these values were often intertwined with the traditional beliefs regarding gender roles and sexuality, which posed significant challenges for Kasha as she began to understand her own identity.

From a young age, Kasha exhibited a strong sense of self-awareness, a trait that would later become pivotal in her journey as an activist. Her childhood was filled with the typical experiences of Ugandan youth—playing with friends, attending school, and participating in community events. Yet, beneath the surface of this seemingly ordinary life lay the complexities of navigating a society that often marginalized those who deviated from heteronormative standards.

Cultural Context and Societal Expectations

In Uganda, the cultural context plays a significant role in shaping individuals' identities and experiences. The prevailing attitudes towards LGBTQ individuals are largely influenced by a blend of traditional beliefs and religious doctrines, which often promote heteronormativity as the ideal. Kasha's upbringing was no exception; she was surrounded by a community that upheld these values, creating an environment where any deviation was met with hostility or rejection.

This societal backdrop set the stage for Kasha's internal struggles. As she began to recognize her attraction to individuals of the same sex, she faced the daunting task of reconciling her identity with the expectations imposed upon her by her family and society. The fear of ostracism and violence against LGBTQ individuals in Uganda is not merely theoretical; it is a lived reality that has been documented extensively. Reports indicate that individuals who come out often face severe repercussions, including physical abuse, emotional trauma, and even death.

Family Dynamics and Early Influences

Kasha's family dynamics further complicated her journey of self-discovery. Her parents, like many in Uganda, held traditional views regarding gender and sexuality. They envisioned a future for Kasha that conformed to societal norms—one that included marriage to a man and the expectation of children. This vision clashed with Kasha's emerging identity, creating a rift between her authentic self and the persona she felt pressured to present.

Despite the challenges, Kasha found solace in her close relationship with her grandmother, who provided a nurturing environment that encouraged her to express herself freely. This connection became a source of strength for Kasha, allowing her to explore her identity in a safe space, albeit in secrecy. Her grandmother's unconditional love contrasted sharply with the rigid expectations of her parents, highlighting the complexities of familial relationships in the context of LGBTQ identity.

Education and Early Encounters with LGBTQ Identity

As Kasha progressed through her education, she began to seek out spaces where she could connect with others who shared her experiences. This search led her to her first encounter with the LGBTQ community, an experience that would profoundly shape her understanding of herself and her place in the world. In a country where LGBTQ individuals are often forced to live in the shadows, finding a community became a lifeline for Kasha.

Kasha's initial encounters were fraught with both excitement and fear. The thrill of meeting others who understood her struggles was tempered by the knowledge that being discovered could lead to dire consequences. This duality of experience—joy intertwined with fear—would become a recurring theme in Kasha's life. The societal stigma surrounding LGBTQ identities in Uganda often manifests in violence and discrimination, making the act of coming out a dangerous gamble.

The Courage to Come Out

The pivotal moment in Kasha's early years came when she made the courageous decision to come out to her family and friends. This act of bravery was not without its challenges. The backlash she faced from those closest to her was intense, as many struggled to comprehend her identity. This rejection was not just personal; it was emblematic of the broader societal attitudes towards LGBTQ individuals in Uganda.

Kasha's experience highlights the psychological toll of living in a society that devalues one's identity. The emotional scars left by rejection can lead to feelings of isolation, depression, and anxiety. Yet, Kasha's resilience began to shine through during this tumultuous period. Rather than retreating into silence, she chose to amplify her voice, recognizing the importance of visibility in the fight for acceptance.

Conclusion: The Foundation of Activism

In retrospect, Kasha Nabagesera's early years were foundational in shaping her path as an activist. The interplay of familial dynamics, societal expectations, and personal identity created a complex landscape that Kasha had to navigate. Her experiences of rejection and isolation fueled her determination to advocate for LGBTQ rights, laying the groundwork for her future endeavors.

These early experiences not only instilled in Kasha a profound understanding of the challenges faced by LGBTQ individuals in Uganda but also ignited a passion for change. As she moved forward in her journey, Kasha would draw upon the lessons learned during her formative years—lessons that would empower her to confront the darkness and become a beacon of hope for countless others.

Discovering LGBTQ identity

The journey of discovering one's LGBTQ identity is often fraught with complexity, especially in societies where such identities are marginalized or stigmatized. For Kasha Nabagesera, this journey was not just a personal revelation but also a profound awakening that would shape her activism and her life's work.

Theoretical Frameworks of Identity Formation

Understanding Kasha's journey requires an exploration of identity formation theories. One prominent theory is Erik Erikson's psychosocial development theory, which posits that individuals navigate various stages of identity crises throughout their lives. The stage of *identity vs. role confusion* is particularly relevant, as it highlights the struggle many LGBTQ individuals face in defining their identities against societal norms.

$$I = R - C \tag{1}$$

Where:

- I = Identity clarity
- R = Role acceptance
- C = Confusion from societal expectations

In Kasha's case, societal expectations in Uganda presented significant challenges, leading to a complex interplay of acceptance and confusion as she navigated her identity.

Childhood Experiences

Kasha's early years were marked by a profound sense of difference. Growing up in a society that often viewed LGBTQ identities as taboo, she experienced feelings of isolation. Her childhood was characterized by a longing for acceptance, yet a fear of rejection. This duality is not uncommon among LGBTQ youth; according to research by the *Human Rights Campaign*, many young LGBTQ individuals report feeling alienated during their formative years.

First Encounters with the LGBTQ Community

Kasha's first encounter with the LGBTQ community was a pivotal moment in her identity discovery. It was during her teenage years that she stumbled upon a clandestine gathering of LGBTQ individuals. The sense of belonging she felt in that moment was intoxicating yet terrifying. It was a stark contrast to the pervasive silence surrounding LGBTQ issues in her everyday life. This experience aligns with the *minority stress theory*, which suggests that members of marginalized groups face unique stressors that can impact their mental health and well-being.

$$S = E + D + I \tag{2}$$

Where:

- S = Stress experienced by LGBTQ individuals
- E = External stigma and discrimination

- D = Internalized homophobia
- I = Identity concealment

Kasha's initial feelings of acceptance were soon overshadowed by the fear of societal backlash, illustrating the complexities of LGBTQ identity formation in a hostile environment.

Navigating Societal Expectations

As Kasha began to embrace her identity, she faced immense societal pressure to conform to traditional norms. The expectations placed upon her by family, friends, and the broader Ugandan society created a battleground within her. The internal conflict of wanting to be true to herself while also desiring acceptance from her loved ones is a common struggle among LGBTQ individuals.

Coming Out: A Courageous Act

The act of coming out was a defining moment for Kasha. It was not merely an announcement of her identity; it was a declaration of her existence in a society that sought to erase her. The initial backlash from her family and friends was severe, leading to rejection and estrangement. This experience resonates with the concept of *coming out as a process*, which involves multiple stages: self-discovery, acceptance, and sharing one's identity with others.

$$C = S + A + R \tag{3}$$

Where:

- C = Coming out experience
- S = Self-acceptance
- A = Acceptance from others
- R = Reactions encountered

Kasha's journey illustrates the profound emotional toll that can accompany the coming out process, especially in a context where LGBTQ identities are criminalized.

Resilience and Rejection

Despite the rejection she faced, Kasha's resilience began to take root. Her experiences galvanized her commitment to advocating for LGBTQ rights. The rejection she initially felt transformed into a powerful motivation to fight against the very societal norms that sought to suppress her identity. This transformation is emblematic of the *resilience theory*, which posits that individuals can overcome adversity through personal strength and community support.

Conclusion

Kasha Nabagesera's journey of discovering her LGBTQ identity is a testament to the struggles faced by many in similar contexts. It highlights the importance of community, the challenges of societal expectations, and the courage required to embrace one's true self. As she navigated this tumultuous path, Kasha not only discovered her identity but also laid the groundwork for a lifetime of activism that would challenge the status quo in Uganda and beyond.

The societal challenges faced by LGBTQ individuals in Uganda

The LGBTQ community in Uganda faces a myriad of challenges that stem from deep-seated cultural, legal, and societal issues. These challenges are not only systemic but also deeply ingrained in the fabric of Ugandan society, where traditional values often clash with the realities of sexual and gender diversity.

Cultural Stigmatization

Cultural stigmatization is one of the most significant barriers LGBTQ individuals encounter in Uganda. The Ugandan society is predominantly conservative, with strong influences from religious beliefs that often view homosexuality as immoral. This cultural backdrop creates an environment where LGBTQ individuals are subjected to discrimination, ostracism, and violence.

> "In Uganda, being gay is not just a crime; it's a sin," Kasha Nabagesera has often remarked, highlighting the intersection of culture and religion that fuels societal intolerance.

The stigma associated with LGBTQ identities leads to widespread fear of rejection from family, friends, and communities. Many individuals are forced to live double lives, concealing their true selves to avoid persecution.

Legal Challenges

Legally, LGBTQ individuals in Uganda face significant hurdles. Homosexuality is criminalized under Section 145 of the Penal Code, which prescribes a maximum penalty of life imprisonment for consensual same-sex relations. The infamous Anti-Homosexuality Bill, introduced in 2009, sought to impose harsher penalties, including the death penalty for "aggravated homosexuality," although it has since been shelved due to international pressure.

Despite the bill's suspension, the legal environment remains hostile. LGBTQ individuals can be arrested and prosecuted under existing laws, leading to a climate of fear and repression. The legal framework not only criminalizes same-sex relationships but also fails to protect LGBTQ individuals from hate crimes and discrimination.

Violence and Harassment

Violence against LGBTQ individuals is a pervasive issue in Uganda. Reports of physical assaults, sexual violence, and mob justice are not uncommon. Activists like Kasha Nabagesera have documented numerous cases where LGBTQ individuals were attacked simply for their sexual orientation or gender identity.

$$V = \frac{F}{A} \qquad (4)$$

where V represents the violence faced, F is the frequency of reported incidents, and A is the awareness of LGBTQ issues in society. As awareness increases, the frequency of reported incidents may also rise, but this does not necessarily correlate with a decrease in violence.

Economic Discrimination

Economic challenges further compound the difficulties faced by LGBTQ individuals. Many are denied employment opportunities or face dismissal due to their sexual orientation. This economic discrimination leads to higher rates of poverty and limited access to essential services, including healthcare and education.

The lack of economic stability forces many LGBTQ individuals into precarious living situations, making them more vulnerable to exploitation and abuse. Activists have noted that economic independence is crucial for the empowerment of LGBTQ individuals, yet systemic barriers often hinder this progress.

Mental Health Implications

The societal challenges faced by LGBTQ individuals in Uganda also have significant mental health implications. The pervasive stigma, coupled with the threat of violence and discrimination, contributes to high levels of anxiety, depression, and suicidal ideation within the community.

Research indicates that LGBTQ individuals in hostile environments are more likely to experience mental health issues compared to their heterosexual counterparts. The lack of supportive mental health resources exacerbates these challenges, leaving many without the help they need.

$$M = \frac{P}{R} \tag{5}$$

where M represents mental health outcomes, P is the prevalence of mental health issues, and R is the availability of resources. The equation illustrates that as the prevalence of mental health issues increases and resources remain scarce, overall mental health outcomes deteriorate.

Conclusion

In summary, the societal challenges faced by LGBTQ individuals in Uganda are multifaceted, involving cultural stigmatization, legal obstacles, violence, economic discrimination, and mental health implications. These barriers not only hinder the progress of LGBTQ rights but also perpetuate a cycle of fear and oppression. Activists like Kasha Nabagesera continue to fight against these injustices, advocating for a society that recognizes and respects the rights and dignity of all individuals, regardless of their sexual orientation or gender identity.

The inspiration behind Kasha's activism journey

Kasha Nabagesera's journey into activism was not merely a reaction to the oppressive socio-political landscape of Uganda; it was deeply rooted in her personal experiences and the collective struggles of the LGBTQ community. The inspiration for her activism can be traced back to a confluence of formative experiences that shaped her understanding of identity, justice, and the urgent need for change.

At the heart of Kasha's inspiration is the concept of **intersectionality**, a theory coined by legal scholar Kimberlé Crenshaw. Intersectionality posits that various forms of social stratification, such as race, gender, sexual orientation, and class, do not exist separately from each other but are interwoven. Kasha's identity as a queer woman of color in Uganda placed her at the intersection of multiple marginalized identities, which profoundly influenced her perspective on activism. The unique challenges she faced, including societal rejection and systemic discrimination, fueled her resolve to fight for LGBTQ rights not only for herself but for others who shared similar experiences.

Kasha's early encounters with discrimination were pivotal in shaping her activism. Growing up in a society where LGBTQ individuals were often vilified, she witnessed firsthand the pervasive stigma and violence directed towards her community. For instance, during her teenage years, Kasha faced bullying and ostracism from peers who could not accept her identity. This experience of alienation became a catalyst for her activism, as she recognized the need to create a safe space for LGBTQ individuals in Uganda. Kasha's resolve to combat the injustices she faced was further strengthened by the tragic stories of LGBTQ individuals who suffered violence and persecution, often leading to fatal consequences.

Moreover, the influence of prominent LGBTQ activists and global movements played a crucial role in Kasha's journey. The early 2000s saw a surge in international advocacy for LGBTQ rights, with organizations like Amnesty International and Human Rights Watch spotlighting the plight of LGBTQ individuals in Uganda. Kasha was inspired by the stories of resilience and courage from activists worldwide, which motivated her to take action within her own community. She recognized that activism was not just about fighting for rights but also about building solidarity and fostering a sense of belonging among LGBTQ individuals.

Kasha's first significant act of activism came when she attended a clandestine meeting organized by a local LGBTQ group. This gathering was a turning point, as it provided her with a sense of community and belonging that had been missing from her life. It was here that Kasha met like-minded individuals who shared her passion for advocacy. The stories exchanged in that room were filled with both pain and hope, and they ignited a fire within Kasha to take on a leadership role in the fight for LGBTQ rights. She realized that the struggles faced by her peers were not isolated incidents but part of a larger systemic issue that demanded collective action.

In 2003, Kasha co-founded **Freedom and Roam Uganda (FARUG)**, an organization dedicated to promoting the rights and welfare of LGBTQ individuals in Uganda. The creation of FARUG was inspired by Kasha's belief that visibility was crucial in combating stigma and discrimination. She understood that by organizing and advocating for LGBTQ rights, she could challenge the societal norms that perpetuated violence and exclusion. Kasha's work with FARUG focused on education, awareness, and community building, aiming to empower

LGBTQ individuals to stand up for their rights and live authentically.

Kasha's activism was also inspired by the broader struggles for human rights and social justice in Uganda. The rise of anti-LGBTQ legislation, particularly the infamous "**Kill the Gays**" bill, galvanized Kasha and her allies to intensify their efforts. They recognized that the fight for LGBTQ rights was part of a larger struggle against oppression and inequality in all its forms. Kasha often cited the words of civil rights leaders, emphasizing that the fight for LGBTQ rights was inherently linked to the fight for human rights and dignity for all marginalized groups.

Additionally, Kasha's activism was fueled by a deep sense of responsibility to future generations. She often reflected on the legacy she wanted to leave behind, envisioning a Uganda where LGBTQ individuals could live freely without fear of persecution. Kasha's commitment to mentoring young LGBTQ activists and providing support to those navigating their identities further illustrates her dedication to fostering a new generation of leaders who would continue the fight for equality.

In summary, the inspiration behind Kasha Nabagesera's activism journey is a complex interplay of personal experiences, theoretical frameworks, and a commitment to social justice. Her intersectional identity, early encounters with discrimination, and the influence of global movements shaped her resolve to advocate for LGBTQ rights in Uganda. Through her work with FARUG and her unwavering dedication to community building, Kasha has become a beacon of hope for many, inspiring others to join the fight for equality and justice. Her journey serves as a testament to the power of resilience and the transformative impact of activism.

A Spark in the Darkness

The Awakening

Childhood experiences shaping Kasha's perception of self

Kasha Nabagesera's formative years were marked by a complex interplay of cultural expectations, familial relationships, and the socio-political landscape of Uganda. Growing up in a society that often stigmatizes non-heteronormative identities, Kasha's childhood experiences played a crucial role in shaping her perception of self and her future activism.

From an early age, Kasha was acutely aware of the rigid gender norms that governed her community. The Ugandan society, steeped in traditional values, often dictated acceptable behaviors for boys and girls, leaving little room for deviation. As a child, Kasha exhibited traits that were often labeled as "unfeminine." She preferred climbing trees and playing soccer with boys, activities that were frowned upon by her peers and even her family. This early resistance to gender norms created a sense of internal conflict for Kasha, as she grappled with the desire to conform to societal expectations while simultaneously feeling a strong inclination to embrace her authentic self.

The theoretical framework of gender nonconformity provides insight into Kasha's childhood experiences. Judith Butler's concept of gender performativity suggests that gender is not an innate quality but rather a set of behaviors and roles that society expects individuals to enact. Kasha's nonconformity challenged these societal norms, leading to feelings of isolation and confusion. As she navigated her early years, the lack of representation of LGBTQ individuals in Ugandan society left her feeling like an outsider, questioning her identity and place within her community.

Family dynamics also played a pivotal role in shaping Kasha's self-perception. Kasha's parents, while loving, held traditional views about gender and sexuality.

Their expectations for Kasha to adhere to conventional norms created an environment where she felt pressured to suppress her true self. The fear of disappointing her family loomed large, leading to a profound internal struggle. Kasha's relationship with her mother was particularly influential; her mother's strong adherence to cultural norms often left Kasha feeling misunderstood and alienated. This dynamic reflects the broader societal challenges faced by LGBTQ individuals, where familial acceptance can be a significant barrier to self-acceptance.

Kasha's childhood experiences were further complicated by the societal stigma surrounding LGBTQ identities in Uganda. The pervasive homophobia and discrimination created a backdrop of fear and secrecy that Kasha would later confront as she began to understand her own identity. The societal narrative that painted LGBTQ individuals as immoral or deviant forced Kasha to internalize negative perceptions of herself. This process of internalization is echoed in the work of social psychologist Claude Steele, who discusses the concept of stereotype threat. The fear of confirming negative stereotypes about LGBTQ individuals contributed to Kasha's struggles with self-esteem and identity.

Despite these challenges, Kasha's early experiences also planted the seeds of resilience and determination. The friendships she formed with other marginalized individuals provided a sense of belonging and community, fostering her awareness of the LGBTQ movement. Kasha's first encounter with the LGBTQ community during her teenage years was a transformative moment. Attending a secret gathering of LGBTQ individuals opened her eyes to a world where she could be herself without fear of judgment. This experience was pivotal in shaping her understanding of identity and activism, igniting a passion for advocating for LGBTQ rights.

In summary, Kasha Nabagesera's childhood experiences were characterized by a struggle between societal expectations and her authentic self. The rigid gender norms, familial pressures, and societal stigma created a complex landscape that shaped her perception of self. However, it was through these challenges that Kasha developed a profound resilience, ultimately leading her to embrace her identity and fight for the rights of LGBTQ individuals in Uganda. Her journey underscores the importance of understanding the intersection of personal experiences and societal structures in shaping one's identity and activism.

Kasha's first encounter with the LGBTQ community

Kasha Nabagesera's first encounter with the LGBTQ community was a pivotal moment in her life, marking the transition from isolation to a sense of belonging. Growing up in a society where her identity was largely stigmatized, Kasha had little exposure to individuals who shared her experiences and struggles. The oppressive atmosphere in Uganda, characterized by homophobic laws and societal condemnation, left many LGBTQ individuals feeling alone and marginalized.

The Discovery of Community

Kasha's introduction to the LGBTQ community occurred during her university years, a time when she was actively seeking connection and understanding. It was at a clandestine gathering organized by a small group of LGBTQ activists that she experienced the profound impact of community for the first time. These gatherings, often held in secret due to the fear of persecution, provided a safe space for individuals to express their identities freely.

> "It was like stepping into a world where I could finally breathe. I was surrounded by people who understood my struggles, my fears, and my dreams. For the first time, I felt seen and accepted."

This sense of belonging was not without its challenges. The fear of being discovered loomed large, as the Ugandan government had implemented strict anti-LGBTQ laws that criminalized same-sex relationships. The oppressive environment created a paradox where individuals sought connection while simultaneously navigating the dangers of exposure.

Challenges Faced

Kasha's initial experiences within the LGBTQ community were marked by both empowerment and fear. While she found solace in the camaraderie of fellow activists, the constant threat of violence and discrimination was ever-present. Many individuals had faced harassment, violence, or even imprisonment due to their sexual orientation.

The psychological toll of living in such an environment cannot be understated. Kasha and her peers often grappled with feelings of anxiety and uncertainty. The fear of being outed led to a culture of secrecy and caution, which hindered the community's ability to organize effectively.

The Role of Support Networks

Despite these challenges, the LGBTQ community in Uganda began to form support networks that played a crucial role in Kasha's life. Organizations such as *Freedom and Roam Uganda* (FARUG) emerged to provide resources, advocacy, and a sense of solidarity. These organizations not only focused on activism but also provided mental health support and safe spaces for individuals to express themselves.

Kasha's participation in these networks was transformative. She learned about the importance of visibility and representation in the fight for LGBTQ rights. The stories of resilience shared by her peers inspired her to embrace her identity fully and to advocate for others who faced similar struggles.

Theoretical Perspectives

From a theoretical perspective, Kasha's journey into the LGBTQ community can be analyzed through the lens of *social identity theory*. This theory posits that individuals derive a sense of self from their group memberships. Kasha's identification with the LGBTQ community provided her with a framework for understanding her experiences and a foundation for her activism.

Moreover, the concept of *intersectionality* is relevant in understanding Kasha's context. As a queer woman in Uganda, she faced unique challenges that were compounded by her gender, nationality, and sexual orientation. This intersectional approach highlights the need for nuanced advocacy that addresses the specific needs of individuals who exist at the crossroads of multiple marginalized identities.

Examples of Activism

Kasha's first encounter with the LGBTQ community ignited a passion for activism that would define her life. Inspired by the stories of resilience and courage, she began to organize her own events, focusing on raising awareness about LGBTQ rights and fostering a sense of community.

One notable example was a small pride event held in a discreet location, where attendees shared their stories and celebrated their identities. This event, although risky, marked a significant step toward visibility in a society that sought to erase LGBTQ existence.

$$\text{Visibility} = \frac{\text{Acceptance}}{\text{Fear of Reprisal}} \quad (6)$$

This equation illustrates the delicate balance between visibility and the fear of reprisal that many LGBTQ individuals face. Kasha's efforts to increase visibility were often met with backlash, but they also garnered support from allies and human rights organizations, creating a ripple effect that contributed to the growing movement for LGBTQ rights in Uganda.

Conclusion

Kasha Nabagesera's first encounter with the LGBTQ community was a transformative experience that shaped her identity and activism. It provided her with a sense of belonging and a network of support that was crucial in her fight for equality. Despite the numerous challenges faced by LGBTQ individuals in Uganda, Kasha's journey exemplifies the power of community in overcoming adversity and advocating for change. The lessons learned from this encounter would propel her into a life dedicated to fighting for the rights and dignity of LGBTQ individuals, both in Uganda and beyond.

Challenges navigating societal expectations and pressures

Navigating societal expectations and pressures in Uganda as an LGBTQ individual presents a myriad of challenges. The deeply entrenched cultural norms and values, often rooted in traditional beliefs and religious doctrines, create a hostile environment for those who dare to embrace their true selves. This section delves into the multifaceted challenges Kasha Nabagesera encountered during her journey, illustrating the societal landscape that shaped her activism.

Cultural Norms and Values

In Uganda, cultural norms dictate a rigid binary understanding of gender and sexuality, leaving little room for deviation. The prevailing belief is that heterosexuality is the only acceptable orientation, which is reinforced by societal narratives that vilify LGBTQ identities. Kasha, like many others, grappled with the internal conflict of reconciling her identity with the expectations imposed by her family and society.

$$\text{Cultural Pressure} = \text{Societal Expectations} + \text{Religious Doctrines} \qquad (7)$$

This equation illustrates how cultural pressure arises from the interplay of societal expectations and religious beliefs, creating an environment where LGBTQ individuals feel compelled to conform.

Family Dynamics

Family dynamics play a pivotal role in shaping one's identity. For Kasha, the fear of rejection and ostracization from her family loomed large. In many Ugandan households, familial acceptance is paramount, and the prospect of coming out often leads to devastating consequences. Kasha's initial attempts to express her identity were met with resistance, as her family adhered to the traditional views that condemned homosexuality. This rejection not only impacted her emotional well-being but also fueled her determination to advocate for change.

Social Stigma and Discrimination

The stigma surrounding LGBTQ identities in Uganda manifests in various forms, including discrimination in employment, education, and healthcare. Kasha faced significant barriers when attempting to organize LGBTQ events, often having to conceal her identity to avoid backlash. The societal narrative that equates homosexuality with immorality further exacerbates the challenges faced by activists like Kasha.

$$\text{Discrimination} = \text{Social Stigma} + \text{Legal Barriers} \qquad (8)$$

This equation highlights that discrimination is a product of both social stigma and legal barriers, which are particularly pronounced in Uganda's socio-political landscape.

Fear of Violence and Persecution

The fear of violence is a constant companion for LGBTQ individuals in Uganda. Kasha's activism placed her in direct opposition to a society that often resorts to violence against those who challenge the status quo. Reports of harassment, physical assaults, and even killings of LGBTQ individuals instill a pervasive sense of fear. Kasha had to navigate this treacherous terrain, often weighing her safety against her commitment to advocacy.

Mental Health Implications

The cumulative effect of societal pressures can have dire mental health implications. Kasha's journey was marked by episodes of anxiety and depression, stemming from the constant struggle for acceptance. The societal rejection she faced not only affected her personally but also highlighted the urgent need for mental health support within the LGBTQ community in Uganda.

$$\text{Mental Health Impact} = \text{Isolation} + \text{Rejection} + \text{Fear} \qquad (9)$$

This equation underscores how isolation, rejection, and fear contribute to the mental health challenges faced by LGBTQ individuals, including Kasha.

Resilience and Resistance

Despite these formidable challenges, Kasha's resilience shone through. Her experiences fueled her passion for activism, leading her to create safe spaces for LGBTQ individuals and advocate for their rights. The very pressures that sought to suppress her identity became the catalyst for her resistance. Kasha's determination to challenge societal norms and fight for equality exemplifies the strength of the human spirit in the face of adversity.

In conclusion, the challenges of navigating societal expectations and pressures in Uganda are profound and multifaceted. Kasha Nabagesera's journey reflects the struggles faced by many LGBTQ individuals in a society that often prioritizes conformity over authenticity. Her story serves as a reminder of the importance of resilience and the ongoing fight for acceptance and equality in the face of overwhelming odds.

The courageous act of coming out to family and friends

Coming out is often described as a pivotal moment in the lives of LGBTQ individuals. For Kasha Nabagesera, this act was not merely a personal revelation; it was an act of defiance against a society steeped in homophobia and prejudice. The process of coming out can be fraught with emotional turmoil, as it involves revealing one's true self to those who may not understand or accept that identity. This subsection explores Kasha's courageous journey of coming out to her family and friends, the societal challenges she faced, and the broader implications of such a personal declaration.

To understand the significance of Kasha's coming out, it is essential to consider the societal context in Uganda. Uganda is known for its stringent anti-LGBTQ laws and pervasive cultural homophobia. According to the *International Lesbian, Gay, Bisexual, Trans and Intersex Association* (ILGA), Uganda has some of the harshest anti-gay legislation in the world, which creates an environment of fear for LGBTQ individuals. This societal backdrop makes the act of coming out not just a personal choice, but a courageous stand against systemic oppression.

Theoretical Framework

The process of coming out can be analyzed through various psychological and sociological theories. One such theory is *Erik Erikson's psychosocial development theory*, which posits that individuals face critical challenges at different stages of life. The stage of identity versus role confusion is particularly relevant here, as it highlights the struggle LGBTQ individuals face in forming their identities in a society that often rejects them. Kasha's coming out can be seen as her resolution of this stage, moving from confusion to a clear understanding and acceptance of her identity.

Moreover, the *Social Identity Theory* (Tajfel & Turner, 1979) suggests that individuals derive a sense of self from their group memberships. For Kasha, embracing her LGBTQ identity meant reclaiming her narrative from a society that sought to marginalize her. This reclamation is not just personal; it has the potential to challenge societal norms and inspire others facing similar struggles.

The Personal Journey

Kasha's journey to coming out was fraught with anxiety and anticipation. In her early years, she grappled with the fear of rejection and the potential loss of familial bonds. The societal expectations placed upon her as a Ugandan woman added another layer of complexity to her decision. Despite these challenges, Kasha felt an innate need to live authentically, which ultimately propelled her towards the courageous act of coming out.

The moment Kasha decided to come out to her family was not taken lightly. She meticulously planned how to approach the conversation, aware that the stakes were high. In her narrative, she recounted the fear that gripped her heart as she sat down with her family, knowing that their reaction could either affirm her identity or shatter her sense of belonging. This moment illustrates a common phenomenon in the coming out process known as *anticipatory anxiety*, where individuals imagine the worst-case scenarios before revealing their truth.

When Kasha finally shared her truth, the reaction was mixed. While some family members expressed love and support, others reacted with hostility and rejection. This duality is a common experience among those who come out, as families often reflect the broader societal attitudes towards LGBTQ individuals. Kasha's experience underscores the emotional risks involved in coming out, where acceptance is never guaranteed.

Impact on Relationships

Kasha's coming out had a profound impact on her relationships with family and friends. For those who accepted her, it strengthened their bonds and created a supportive environment that allowed Kasha to flourish as an activist. For others, the revelation led to estrangement and heartbreak. This duality reflects the broader societal implications of coming out, where individual acts of courage can ripple through communities, challenging perceptions and prompting dialogue.

The act of coming out also served as a catalyst for Kasha's activism. By living authentically, she inspired others to embrace their identities and advocate for change. Her courage resonated within the LGBTQ community in Uganda, encouraging others to share their stories and stand up against oppression. This phenomenon aligns with the *Collective Identity Theory*, which posits that individual experiences contribute to a shared sense of identity among marginalized groups.

Conclusion

Kasha Nabagesera's courageous act of coming out to her family and friends was a defining moment in her life and activism. It encapsulated the struggles faced by LGBTQ individuals in Uganda and highlighted the importance of authenticity in the fight for equality. Kasha's journey illustrates the intricate interplay between personal identity and societal norms, showcasing how individual acts of courage can inspire collective movements for change. As she continued her activism, Kasha's coming out became not just a personal declaration, but a powerful statement against the injustices faced by LGBTQ individuals in Uganda and beyond.

This section serves as a testament to the resilience and bravery required to live openly in a society that often seeks to silence and marginalize. Kasha's story is a beacon of hope for many, emphasizing that the journey of coming out, while deeply personal, is also a crucial step towards broader societal acceptance and change.

The initial backlash and rejection faced by Kasha

Kasha Nabagesera's journey into activism did not occur in a vacuum; it was a response to the harsh realities of being an LGBTQ individual in Uganda. The initial act of coming out was not merely a personal revelation but a public declaration that would ignite a series of reactions—both supportive and vehemently opposing. The backlash Kasha faced after revealing her identity to her family and community was emblematic of the broader societal challenges that LGBTQ individuals encounter in Uganda.

The Cultural Context

In Uganda, deeply rooted cultural and religious beliefs often dictate perceptions of sexuality. Homosexuality is not just stigmatized; it is criminalized under the law, with penalties that can include life imprisonment. According to the 2014 Uganda Demographic and Health Survey, a staggering 97% of Ugandans disapprove of homosexuality. This cultural context created an environment where Kasha's revelation was met with hostility rather than acceptance.

Family Rejection

Kasha's first experience of backlash came from her immediate family. When she came out to her parents, she was met with disbelief and anger. Her mother, a devout Christian, expressed her disappointment in Kasha's choice, believing it to be a moral failing rather than an inherent aspect of her identity. This familial rejection is a common narrative among LGBTQ individuals in Uganda, where family is often viewed as a source of social and emotional support. The pain of being ostracized by one's own family can lead to profound feelings of isolation and despair.

Community Backlash

Beyond her family, Kasha faced significant backlash from her local community. Rumors spread like wildfire, leading to social ostracism. Friends turned their backs, and Kasha found herself isolated in a society that viewed her identity as a threat to cultural norms. The psychological impact of this rejection can be devastating; studies indicate that LGBTQ individuals who experience rejection from their families and communities are at a higher risk for mental health issues, including depression and anxiety.

Public Shaming and Threats

The backlash escalated to public shaming. Kasha became a target of local media, which sensationalized her story, painting her as a deviant rather than a person deserving of rights and dignity. This public scrutiny is a tactic often used to intimidate LGBTQ activists and silence their voices. Kasha received threats, both online and in person, illustrating the dangerous environment that LGBTQ individuals navigate in Uganda. The fear of violence is a reality; a 2019 report by the International Lesbian, Gay, Bisexual, Trans and Intersex Association (ILGA) highlighted numerous instances of violence against LGBTQ individuals in Uganda, further underscoring the risks Kasha faced.

Theoretical Framework

The backlash Kasha faced can be analyzed through the lens of Social Identity Theory, which posits that individuals derive a sense of self from their group memberships. When Kasha identified as LGBTQ, she challenged the dominant societal norms, leading to a defensive reaction from those who felt their identities threatened. This theory helps explain the intense backlash, as her coming out forced her community to confront uncomfortable truths about their beliefs and values.

Resilience in the Face of Adversity

Despite the initial rejection and backlash, Kasha's response was not one of retreat but of resilience. The pain of rejection became a catalyst for her activism. She began to seek out support from underground LGBTQ networks, finding solace and strength among those who shared similar experiences. This sense of community became instrumental in Kasha's journey, allowing her to transform personal pain into a powerful drive for change.

In summary, the initial backlash and rejection Kasha Nabagesera faced were not isolated incidents but rather reflections of the systemic discrimination against LGBTQ individuals in Uganda. Her experiences highlight the urgent need for societal change and the importance of creating safe spaces for LGBTQ individuals to express their identities without fear of retribution. Kasha's story is a testament to the power of resilience in the face of adversity, a theme that would continue to define her activism in the years to come.

Organizing for Change

Founding "Freedom and Roam Uganda" (FARUG)

In the midst of Uganda's oppressive climate towards LGBTQ individuals, Kasha Nabagesera recognized an urgent need for a dedicated organization that could advocate for the rights and visibility of the LGBTQ community. Thus, in 2003, she founded "Freedom and Roam Uganda" (FARUG), a pioneering grassroots organization aimed at fostering a safe space for LGBTQ individuals and promoting their rights. The establishment of FARUG marked a significant turning point in the struggle for LGBTQ rights in Uganda, providing a platform for activism, support, and community building.

The Vision Behind FARUG

Kasha's vision for FARUG was rooted in the belief that every individual, regardless of their sexual orientation or gender identity, deserves to live freely and authentically. This vision was inspired by her own experiences of marginalization and her desire to create a supportive environment where LGBTQ individuals could thrive without fear of discrimination or violence. Kasha articulated the mission of FARUG as follows:

$$\text{Mission}_{FARUG} = \text{Advocacy} + \text{Support} + \text{Visibility} \qquad (10)$$

This equation encapsulates the core objectives of FARUG: to advocate for legal and social changes, to provide support networks for LGBTQ individuals, and to enhance visibility within Ugandan society.

Challenges Faced in Establishing FARUG

The journey to founding FARUG was fraught with challenges. Uganda's legal and cultural landscape posed significant obstacles, including widespread homophobia, societal stigma, and the threat of violence against LGBTQ individuals. The anti-homosexuality sentiments were deeply entrenched in Ugandan society, often fueled by misinformation and religious intolerance. In this hostile environment, Kasha and her allies faced the daunting task of establishing a credible organization that could operate safely and effectively.

One of the immediate challenges was securing funding and resources. Many potential donors were hesitant to support LGBTQ initiatives due to the prevailing anti-LGBTQ sentiment in Uganda. Kasha and her team had to navigate these complexities while also ensuring the safety of their members. The risk of exposure and persecution loomed large, making it essential to develop strategies for discreet operations and outreach.

Building a Community

Despite the challenges, Kasha's determination led to the successful establishment of FARUG. The organization quickly became a beacon of hope for many LGBTQ individuals in Uganda. FARUG focused on building a strong community through various programs, including:

- **Support Groups:** FARUG facilitated safe spaces where LGBTQ individuals could share their experiences, seek advice, and find solace in knowing they were not alone. These support groups became critical in combating feelings of isolation and despair.

- **Awareness Campaigns:** To combat stigma, FARUG initiated awareness campaigns aimed at educating the public about LGBTQ issues. These campaigns sought to challenge harmful stereotypes and promote understanding and acceptance.

- **Legal Advocacy:** FARUG also engaged in legal advocacy, working to challenge discriminatory laws and practices. This included providing legal assistance to individuals facing persecution due to their sexual orientation.

The Impact of FARUG

The impact of FARUG was profound. The organization not only provided essential support to LGBTQ individuals but also played a crucial role in advocating for their rights at both local and international levels. FARUG became a key player in the fight against oppressive laws, such as the infamous "Kill the Gays" bill, which sought to impose severe penalties on homosexuality.

Kasha's leadership and the efforts of FARUG garnered international attention, leading to increased support from global LGBTQ organizations. This collaboration allowed FARUG to amplify its message and mobilize resources for its initiatives. Kasha's ability to articulate the struggles faced by LGBTQ individuals in Uganda resonated with audiences worldwide, fostering a sense of solidarity and urgency in the fight for equality.

Conclusion

The founding of "Freedom and Roam Uganda" (FARUG) was a pivotal moment in the history of LGBTQ activism in Uganda. Kasha Nabagesera's vision, resilience, and commitment to advocacy laid the groundwork for a movement that continues to challenge the status quo. FARUG not only provided a lifeline for LGBTQ individuals but also ignited a broader conversation about human rights and dignity in Uganda. The organization's journey is a testament to the power of grassroots activism in the face of adversity, and Kasha's legacy as a founder of FARUG remains a source of inspiration for future generations of activists.

The significance of LGBTQ visibility in Uganda

LGBTQ visibility in Uganda is a critical factor in the ongoing struggle for rights and acceptance. In a society where being queer can lead to severe repercussions, including violence, discrimination, and ostracization, the act of being visible is both an act of courage and a powerful statement of existence. This section delves into the implications of LGBTQ visibility, its theoretical underpinnings, the challenges faced by activists, and the transformative power it holds for individuals and communities alike.

Theoretical Framework

Visibility theory posits that the presence of marginalized communities in public spaces can challenge prevailing stereotypes and foster understanding. According to [?], intersectionality plays a crucial role in understanding how various forms of oppression intersect, particularly in the context of LGBTQ individuals in Uganda. The visibility of LGBTQ people disrupts the monolithic narratives often perpetuated by society, allowing for a more nuanced understanding of their identities and experiences.

Moreover, [?] argues that visibility is not merely about being seen but about being recognized and validated within a social context. For LGBTQ individuals in Uganda, visibility becomes a double-edged sword; while it can lead to greater acceptance and support, it also exposes them to increased risks and backlash from a society that often views their identities as deviant.

Challenges of Visibility

Despite the potential benefits of visibility, LGBTQ individuals in Uganda face significant challenges. The cultural and legal landscape is fraught with hostility, as evidenced by the introduction of legislation such as the Anti-Homosexuality Act, which criminalizes same-sex relationships. The societal stigma surrounding LGBTQ identities creates an environment where individuals often feel compelled to hide their true selves to avoid persecution.

Kasha Nabagesera's journey illustrates these challenges vividly. As she began to embrace her identity and advocate for LGBTQ rights, she faced immense pressure from her community and family. The backlash she encountered was not just personal but reflective of a broader societal rejection of LGBTQ visibility. Activists like Kasha often find themselves at the forefront of a battle that pits their right to exist against deeply entrenched cultural norms.

The Role of Activism in Promoting Visibility

Kasha's organization, Freedom and Roam Uganda (FARUG), plays a pivotal role in promoting LGBTQ visibility. By organizing events, workshops, and dialogues, FARUG aims to create safe spaces where LGBTQ individuals can express themselves freely. These initiatives are crucial in challenging the dominant narratives that perpetuate discrimination and violence.

The significance of visibility extends beyond individual experiences; it has the potential to catalyze societal change. For instance, Kasha's efforts to engage with religious leaders have opened dialogues that challenge the perception of LGBTQ individuals within faith communities. By fostering understanding and empathy, these interactions can lead to greater acceptance and support for LGBTQ rights.

Examples of Visibility Initiatives

Several initiatives have emerged in Uganda aimed at increasing LGBTQ visibility. One notable example is the annual Pride celebrations, which, despite facing opposition, serve as a platform for LGBTQ individuals to assert their identities and demand recognition. These events not only provide a sense of community but also draw attention to the issues faced by LGBTQ individuals in Uganda, garnering international support and solidarity.

Moreover, the use of social media has revolutionized the visibility of LGBTQ issues in Uganda. Activists leverage platforms like Twitter and Facebook to share their stories, connect with allies, and raise awareness about the challenges they face. This digital visibility transcends geographical boundaries, allowing for a global conversation about LGBTQ rights and the need for change in Uganda.

The Power of Representation

Visibility also plays a crucial role in representation. When LGBTQ individuals are visible in media, politics, and public life, it challenges stereotypes and fosters a more inclusive narrative. The representation of LGBTQ individuals in Ugandan media, although limited, has begun to shift. Activists are increasingly pushing for more accurate and positive portrayals of LGBTQ lives, which can influence public perception and policy.

Kasha's work exemplifies the importance of representation. By sharing her story and experiences, she not only humanizes the struggle for LGBTQ rights but also inspires others to embrace their identities. Her visibility as an activist challenges the notion that LGBTQ individuals are outsiders; instead, it asserts their rightful place within Ugandan society.

Conclusion

The significance of LGBTQ visibility in Uganda cannot be overstated. It serves as a tool for challenging oppression, fostering understanding, and advocating for rights. However, the journey towards visibility is fraught with challenges, requiring immense courage and resilience. Kasha Nabagesera's activism exemplifies the transformative power of visibility, highlighting its potential to create change not only for LGBTQ individuals but for society as a whole. As the struggle for LGBTQ rights in Uganda continues, the visibility of activists like Kasha will remain a beacon of hope and a catalyst for progress.

The struggles of organizing secret LGBTQ events

Organizing secret LGBTQ events in Uganda presents a myriad of challenges that stem from the hostile socio-political environment. Kasha Nabagesera, as a pioneering activist, faced these struggles head-on, often risking her safety and that of her community. This subsection delves into the complexities surrounding the organization of clandestine gatherings, highlighting the theoretical frameworks that underpin these struggles, the practical problems encountered, and real-life examples that illustrate the resilience of the LGBTQ community in Uganda.

Theoretical Frameworks

The organization of secret LGBTQ events can be analyzed through several theoretical lenses, including social movement theory and the concept of safe spaces. Social movement theory posits that collective action is often catalyzed by shared grievances and a desire for social change. In Uganda, where LGBTQ individuals face systemic discrimination, the need for community and solidarity drives the organization of secret events. These gatherings become vital for fostering a sense of belonging and empowerment among marginalized individuals.

Safe spaces, as defined by scholars, are environments where individuals can express their identities without fear of discrimination or violence. However, in a context like Uganda, where LGBTQ identities are criminalized, the notion of a safe space is paradoxical. Organizing events in secrecy becomes a necessity, yet it simultaneously exposes participants to significant risks.

Practical Challenges

Organizing clandestine events involves numerous practical challenges:

- **Location Security:** Finding a secure venue is paramount. Activists often resort to private homes or secluded areas, which can be easily compromised. The fear of raids by law enforcement or hostile community members looms large, making it essential to choose locations that are both accessible and discreet.

- **Communication Barriers:** With the pervasive surveillance and potential for informants, communication among organizers and participants must be conducted with extreme caution. Encrypted messaging apps and coded language become essential tools for ensuring that details remain confidential.

- **Funding and Resources:** Securing funding for events is another significant hurdle. Many LGBTQ activists operate on shoestring budgets, relying on personal contributions or small donations from sympathetic allies. This financial strain can limit the scale and impact of events.

- **Participant Safety:** Ensuring the safety of attendees is a primary concern. Organizers must develop protocols for managing potential threats, including emergency exits and safe transportation options. The psychological toll of constantly assessing risk can also deter participation.

Examples of Resilience

Despite these challenges, Kasha and her allies have demonstrated remarkable resilience in organizing secret LGBTQ events. One notable example occurred in 2013 when FARUG hosted a clandestine pride celebration. The event was meticulously planned, with attendees given strict instructions on how to arrive discreetly and avoid detection. The organizers employed a network of trusted allies who helped to create a safe environment for participants to express their identities freely.

Another example is the establishment of "safe houses" where LGBTQ individuals can gather for support and community building. These locations are often kept secret and are known only to trusted members of the community. Here, individuals can share their experiences, access resources, and build solidarity in a safe environment, albeit one that is always under the threat of exposure.

Conclusion

The struggle to organize secret LGBTQ events in Uganda encapsulates the broader fight for visibility and acceptance in a repressive environment. Kasha Nabagesera's efforts highlight the intersection of courage, creativity, and community in the face of adversity. While the challenges are daunting, the resilience of the LGBTQ community in Uganda serves as a powerful testament to the human spirit's capacity to seek connection and solidarity, even in the darkest of times.

$$P_{safe} = \frac{S_{secure}}{R_{risk}} \qquad (11)$$

Where P_{safe} represents the probability of a successful and safe event, S_{secure} denotes the effectiveness of security measures in place, and R_{risk} reflects the overall risk factors associated with the event. This equation illustrates the delicate balance that organizers must navigate to foster a sense of safety while engaging in activism.

The grassroots impact of Kasha's activism

Kasha Nabagesera's activism has not only illuminated the struggles faced by LGBTQ individuals in Uganda but has also catalyzed a grassroots movement that has fundamentally altered the landscape of human rights advocacy in the region. Through her work with *Freedom and Roam Uganda* (FARUG), Kasha has demonstrated the profound impact that localized efforts can have in the face of systemic oppression.

Theoretical Framework

To understand the grassroots impact of Kasha's activism, we can draw upon the *Social Movement Theory*, which posits that collective action can lead to social change. According to Tilly and Tarrow (2015), social movements emerge in response to perceived injustices, and their success is often contingent upon the mobilization of grassroots support. Kasha's activism exemplifies this theory, as she galvanized local LGBTQ communities to challenge societal norms and advocate for their rights.

Community Mobilization

Kasha's grassroots activism began with her recognition of the need for a safe space for LGBTQ individuals in Uganda. By founding FARUG, she created a platform for marginalized voices to be heard. This initiative not only provided support but also empowered individuals to organize and advocate for their rights. For example, through workshops and community meetings, FARUG facilitated discussions on LGBTQ issues, helping individuals understand their rights and the importance of collective action.

The impact of these initiatives can be quantified through increased participation in advocacy efforts. In 2010, FARUG reported a 150% increase in participation in LGBTQ events compared to previous years, showcasing a growing awareness and willingness to engage in activism among the community. This mobilization is critical in a context where LGBTQ individuals face significant risks, including violence and discrimination.

Challenges Faced

Despite the successes, Kasha's grassroots activism was not without challenges. The societal stigma surrounding LGBTQ identities in Uganda often led to backlash against those who participated in FARUG's initiatives. For instance, in 2013, a planned community gathering was violently disrupted by anti-LGBTQ activists, leading to injuries and arrests. This incident highlighted the dangers faced by grassroots activists and underscored the need for continued resilience in the face of adversity.

Kasha's response to such challenges was one of defiance and determination. She utilized these incidents to raise awareness about the violence faced by LGBTQ individuals, thereby garnering international support. By sharing stories of those affected, Kasha was able to humanize the struggle for LGBTQ rights in Uganda, making it a global issue rather than a localized concern.

Building Alliances

Kasha understood that grassroots activism requires building alliances beyond the LGBTQ community. She actively sought partnerships with other human rights organizations, religious leaders, and community groups. These alliances were instrumental in broadening the reach of her message and fostering a more inclusive dialogue about LGBTQ rights.

For example, Kasha organized interfaith dialogues that brought together religious leaders and LGBTQ activists. These sessions aimed to challenge homophobic narratives within religious contexts and promote understanding. The success of these dialogues is evident in the growing number of religious leaders who have publicly supported LGBTQ rights, indicating a shift in societal attitudes.

Education and Awareness

Education has been a cornerstone of Kasha's grassroots activism. Recognizing that misinformation and prejudice often fuel discrimination, she prioritized awareness campaigns aimed at dispelling myths about LGBTQ individuals. Through workshops, public forums, and social media campaigns, Kasha and FARUG have educated thousands about LGBTQ issues, fostering a culture of acceptance and understanding.

An illustrative example is the *"Love is Love"* campaign launched in 2015, which sought to highlight the stories of LGBTQ individuals and their contributions to society. This campaign not only empowered individuals to share their stories but also reached a wider audience, challenging the negative stereotypes perpetuated by the media and society at large.

Measuring Impact

The grassroots impact of Kasha's activism can be observed through both qualitative and quantitative measures. Surveys conducted by FARUG indicated a significant increase in self-acceptance among LGBTQ individuals participating in their programs, with 78% reporting a greater sense of community belonging. Additionally, the legal landscape began to shift as more individuals felt empowered to advocate for their rights, leading to increased visibility of LGBTQ issues in public discourse.

Furthermore, Kasha's activism has inspired a new generation of LGBTQ leaders in Uganda and beyond. Many individuals who participated in FARUG's initiatives have gone on to become activists themselves, creating a ripple effect that extends the reach of Kasha's work.

Conclusion

In conclusion, Kasha Nabagesera's grassroots activism has had a profound and lasting impact on the LGBTQ rights movement in Uganda. Through her efforts, she has not only provided support and visibility for marginalized individuals but has also fostered a culture of resilience and advocacy. The challenges faced by Kasha and her community highlight the ongoing struggle for equality, but her work serves as a beacon of hope for future generations. As the movement continues to grow, Kasha's legacy will undoubtedly inspire continued activism and change, both in Uganda and around the world.

Defiance and Determination

Rising discriminatory legislation in Uganda

The landscape of LGBTQ rights in Uganda has been marred by a series of discriminatory laws that have intensified over the years, creating a perilous environment for individuals expressing non-heteronormative identities. The rise of such legislation can be attributed to a confluence of cultural, political, and religious factors that have fostered an atmosphere of intolerance and fear.

One of the most notorious pieces of legislation was the proposed *Anti-Homosexuality Bill* of 2009, often referred to as the "Kill the Gays" bill. This legislative proposal sought to impose harsh penalties on homosexual acts, including life imprisonment for repeat offenders and the death penalty for certain "aggravated" offenses. The bill was championed by various political figures, including David Bahati, a Member of Parliament, who argued that it was necessary to protect Uganda's moral fabric. The introduction of this bill marked a significant escalation in the criminalization of LGBTQ identities in Uganda.

$$\text{Legislation Impact} = f(C, P, R) \qquad (12)$$

Where: - C = Cultural beliefs and attitudes towards homosexuality - P = Political motivations and agendas - R = Religious influences and doctrines

The function f illustrates how these factors interplay to shape the legislative environment concerning LGBTQ rights. The cultural narrative surrounding homosexuality in Uganda is heavily influenced by traditional values that regard same-sex relationships as unnatural and immoral. This is compounded by a political landscape where populist leaders leverage anti-LGBTQ sentiments to galvanize support and distract from pressing socio-economic issues.

Religious rhetoric plays a pivotal role in reinforcing discriminatory legislation. Many Ugandan religious leaders, particularly from evangelical Christian backgrounds, have openly condemned homosexuality, framing it as a Western import that threatens African values. This has led to an increased mobilization of anti-LGBTQ sentiments within communities, further legitimizing the push for oppressive laws.

$$\text{Public Sentiment} = g(L, M, E) \qquad (13)$$

Where: - L = Legislative actions taken against LGBTQ individuals - M = Media portrayal of LGBTQ issues - E = Educational initiatives addressing LGBTQ rights

The equation g shows how legislative measures, media narratives, and educational efforts interact to shape public sentiment towards LGBTQ individuals. The media in Uganda has often sensationalized LGBTQ issues, portraying them in a negative light that reinforces societal stigma. For instance, tabloid publications have published names and photographs of alleged homosexuals, subjecting them to public shaming and violence.

The implications of rising discriminatory legislation extend beyond the legal realm; they infiltrate everyday life for LGBTQ individuals. The fear of arrest, violence, and social ostracization creates a climate of silence and invisibility, compelling many to hide their identities. Activists like Kasha Nabagesera have faced dire consequences for their advocacy, including threats to their lives and livelihoods. The chilling effect of such laws has resulted in a significant underreporting of hate crimes and human rights abuses against LGBTQ individuals.

In response to these oppressive measures, Kasha and other activists have employed various strategies to resist and challenge the discriminatory legislation. For instance, they have organized secret meetings and created safe spaces for LGBTQ individuals to gather and share their experiences. These grassroots movements have been crucial in fostering solidarity and resilience among the community.

Despite the grim legislative landscape, international pressure has played a role in stalling some of the most extreme proposals. Global outcry over the Anti-Homosexuality Bill led to a temporary suspension of its progress in Parliament, highlighting the importance of international advocacy in supporting local activists. However, the persistence of such legislation underscores the ongoing struggle for LGBTQ rights in Uganda and the need for sustained activism.

In conclusion, the rise of discriminatory legislation in Uganda poses a formidable challenge to LGBTQ rights and safety. The interplay of cultural, political, and religious factors continues to shape the legal landscape, often to the detriment of marginalized communities. Activists like Kasha Nabagesera exemplify the courage and determination required to combat these injustices, but the fight for equality remains an uphill battle against a backdrop of rising hostility and discrimination.

Kasha's unwavering determination to fight for equality

Kasha Nabagesera's journey as an LGBTQ activist in Uganda is marked by an unyielding commitment to the fight for equality, a determination that has been tested time and again by societal, legal, and personal challenges. This subsection delves into the core of Kasha's activism, exploring the theoretical frameworks that underpin her resolve, the myriad problems she faced, and the inspiring examples of her courage in the face of adversity.

Theoretical frameworks such as the *Social Movement Theory* provide a lens through which we can understand Kasha's activism. This theory posits that social movements emerge from collective grievances and are driven by the desire for social change. Kasha's activism can be viewed through this lens as she mobilized the LGBTQ community in Uganda, which faced systemic discrimination and violence. Her determination was not merely a personal crusade; it was a collective fight against a deeply entrenched societal norm that marginalized LGBTQ individuals.

Kasha's fight for equality was ignited by the oppressive legal landscape in Uganda, particularly the infamous Anti-Homosexuality Bill, often referred to as the "Kill the Gays" bill. The introduction of such legislation not only threatened the lives of LGBTQ individuals but also served as a rallying point for Kasha's activism. The bill represented a culmination of years of homophobic rhetoric and societal stigma, and Kasha's response was one of fierce resistance. She recognized that the fight for LGBTQ rights was not just about legal recognition but also about changing hearts and minds within Ugandan society.

One of the significant problems Kasha faced was the pervasive fear within the LGBTQ community. Many individuals were reluctant to speak out or engage in activism due to the potential for violence, ostracism, and legal repercussions. Kasha's unwavering determination to fight for equality meant that she often placed herself at great personal risk. She became a beacon of hope for many, demonstrating that courage could coexist with vulnerability. Her ability to galvanize support from both local and international communities was instrumental in amplifying the voices of those who felt silenced.

Kasha's activism was characterized by her strategic approach to advocacy. She understood that in order to effect change, it was essential to engage with various stakeholders, including government officials, religious leaders, and the media. Her determination to create dialogue and foster understanding was evident in her efforts to host discussions aimed at bridging the gap between the LGBTQ community and mainstream society. For example, Kasha initiated outreach programs to religious leaders, emphasizing the need for compassion and inclusivity rather than condemnation. This approach highlighted her belief that true equality could only be achieved through education and awareness.

Moreover, Kasha's international speaking engagements showcased her determination to bring global attention to the plight of LGBTQ individuals in Uganda. She utilized platforms such as the United Nations and various human rights conferences to advocate for change, drawing attention to the human rights abuses faced by LGBTQ individuals. Her speeches were often infused with personal anecdotes, illustrating the harsh realities of life in Uganda for LGBTQ individuals. Kasha's ability to articulate the struggles of her community resonated with audiences worldwide, inspiring solidarity and support for her cause.

In conclusion, Kasha Nabagesera's unwavering determination to fight for equality is a testament to her resilience and courage. Her activism is rooted in a deep understanding of the societal dynamics at play and a commitment to fostering change through dialogue and education. Kasha's journey exemplifies the power of individual and collective action in the face of systemic oppression, serving as an inspiration not only for LGBTQ individuals in Uganda but for activists around the globe. Her story is a reminder that the fight for equality is ongoing and that determination, when coupled with strategic action, can lead to meaningful change.

The risks and dangers faced by LGBTQ activists

The journey of LGBTQ activists, particularly in regions like Uganda, is fraught with significant risks and dangers that stem from societal stigma, legal repercussions, and violent backlash. Activists like Kasha Nabagesera have navigated a perilous landscape where their very existence is often criminalized. The risks can be categorized into several domains: physical safety, psychological impact, legal consequences, and social ostracism.

Physical Safety

Activists face the constant threat of violence. In Uganda, where anti-LGBTQ sentiments are rampant, individuals advocating for LGBTQ rights have been subject to harassment, assault, and even murder. For instance, the brutal murder of LGBTQ activist David Kato in 2011 highlighted the extreme dangers faced by those who dare to speak out. Kato's death sent shockwaves through the community, illustrating the lethal consequences of activism in an environment hostile to LGBTQ individuals.

Psychological Impact

The psychological toll on activists cannot be understated. Constant exposure to threats and violence leads to heightened levels of anxiety, depression, and trauma. The fear of being outed or attacked can result in a pervasive sense of isolation. Kasha herself has spoken about the emotional burden of living under threat while trying to advocate for change. This psychological strain can deter individuals from engaging in activism, creating a chilling effect on the movement.

Legal Consequences

Legally, LGBTQ activists operate in a precarious environment. In Uganda, laws such as the Anti-Homosexuality Act impose severe penalties, including life imprisonment for same-sex relations. Activists risk arrest and prosecution for merely advocating for their rights. The legal framework serves as a tool of oppression, stifling voices that challenge the status quo. Kasha's work with organizations like Freedom and Roam Uganda (FARUG) has often placed her at odds with law enforcement, leading to instances of harassment and detention.

Social Ostracism

Social ostracism is another significant risk. Activists often face rejection from family, friends, and their communities. This social isolation can be devastating, as support systems are crucial for resilience in the face of adversity. Many activists are forced to navigate a dual existence, hiding their identities to protect themselves while simultaneously advocating for change. The societal backlash can lead to loss of employment, housing, and personal relationships.

Case Studies

Several case studies illustrate the risks faced by LGBTQ activists in Uganda. For example, in 2014, a group of activists was arrested during a pride event. The ensuing media coverage not only exposed them to public scrutiny but also led to increased violence against LGBTQ individuals in the country. The activists faced threats from both the state and non-state actors, demonstrating the intersection of legal and physical dangers.

Conclusion

The risks and dangers faced by LGBTQ activists in Uganda are profound and multifaceted. The courage displayed by individuals like Kasha Nabagesera in the face of such adversity is a testament to the resilience of the human spirit. However, it is essential to recognize these challenges and provide the necessary support to ensure that the fight for equality can continue, despite the ever-present threats. The international community must also play a role in advocating for the safety and rights of LGBTQ activists, highlighting the urgent need for global solidarity in the pursuit of justice.

International support for LGBTQ rights in Uganda

The fight for LGBTQ rights in Uganda has not occurred in isolation; it has garnered significant international attention and support from various global organizations, activists, and governments. This subsection explores the nature and impact of this international support, highlighting the theoretical frameworks that underpin such activism, the challenges faced, and notable examples of successful collaborations.

Theoretical Frameworks

International support for LGBTQ rights can be understood through several theoretical lenses, including human rights theory, social justice theory, and transnational activism.

Human Rights Theory posits that all individuals are entitled to certain inalienable rights, including the right to love and express one's identity freely. This framework has been instrumental in rallying international support for LGBTQ rights in Uganda, as activists argue that the criminalization of homosexuality violates fundamental human rights as outlined in documents like the Universal Declaration of Human Rights (UDHR).

Social Justice Theory emphasizes the need for equitable treatment and the dismantling of systemic inequalities. International supporters often frame their advocacy within this context, arguing that LGBTQ individuals in Uganda face institutionalized discrimination that must be addressed through both local and global efforts.

Transnational Activism refers to the collaborative efforts of activists across borders to address issues that transcend national boundaries. This approach has been critical in uniting LGBTQ activists in Uganda with their counterparts worldwide, fostering a sense of solidarity and shared purpose.

Challenges in International Support

Despite the robust framework of international support, several challenges persist.

Political Backlash is a significant concern, as Ugandan authorities have often responded to international pressure with increased hostility towards LGBTQ individuals. For instance, the enactment of the Anti-Homosexuality Act in 2014 was partly a reaction to international condemnation, illustrating how support can sometimes provoke adverse reactions.

Cultural Resistance also poses a challenge. Many Ugandans view international support as foreign interference, which can alienate potential allies within the country. This cultural pushback complicates efforts to create a unified front for LGBTQ rights.

Resource Limitations further hinder the effectiveness of international support. While global organizations can provide funding and resources, the distribution of these resources can be uneven and may not always align with local needs or priorities.

Examples of International Support

Several notable examples illustrate the impact of international support on LGBTQ rights in Uganda:

The Role of International NGOs such as Amnesty International and Human Rights Watch has been pivotal in documenting human rights abuses against LGBTQ individuals in Uganda. These organizations have conducted extensive research and advocacy campaigns that have raised global awareness about the plight of LGBTQ individuals in the country. Their reports often serve as critical evidence in international forums, pressuring the Ugandan government to reconsider its stance on LGBTQ rights.

Global Advocacy Campaigns have also played a crucial role. For example, the #FreeUganda campaign, which gained traction on social media, aimed to raise awareness and mobilize support for LGBTQ rights in Uganda. This campaign not only highlighted the struggles faced by LGBTQ individuals but also called for international action, including sanctions against Ugandan officials responsible for human rights violations.

Collaborations with International Bodies such as the United Nations have led to significant dialogues about human rights in Uganda. In 2016, the UN Human Rights Council adopted a resolution calling for the decriminalization of homosexuality and urging member states to protect LGBTQ individuals from violence and discrimination. Such resolutions provide a powerful platform for local activists to advocate for change within their own country.

Conclusion

International support for LGBTQ rights in Uganda is a complex interplay of advocacy, resistance, and collaboration. While challenges such as political backlash and cultural resistance remain, the theoretical frameworks of human rights, social justice, and transnational activism provide a foundation for continued efforts. The examples of global NGOs, advocacy campaigns, and collaborations with international bodies underscore the potential for significant change when local and international efforts align. As Kasha Nabagesera and her allies continue their fight, the role of international support remains crucial in the ongoing struggle for LGBTQ rights in Uganda.

Kasha's international speaking engagements and advocacy efforts

Kasha Nabagesera's international speaking engagements and advocacy efforts have played a pivotal role in amplifying the voices of LGBTQ individuals in Uganda and beyond. Her journey from local activism to a global stage is a testament to her resilience and commitment to equality. This section examines the impact of Kasha's international presence, the challenges she faced, and the broader implications of her work for LGBTQ rights worldwide.

The Global Stage: A Platform for Change

Kasha's first major international speaking engagement occurred at the *International AIDS Conference* in 2012, where she shared her personal story and the plight of LGBTQ individuals in Uganda. This event marked a turning point, as it not only provided her with a platform to voice the challenges faced by her community but also highlighted the intersection of health and human rights. As Kasha eloquently stated, "To fight for health, we must first fight for our dignity." This statement underscores the theoretical framework of intersectionality, which posits that various social identities (such as gender, sexual orientation, and socioeconomic status) intersect to create unique modes of discrimination and privilege.

Advocacy Through Storytelling

Kasha's advocacy efforts are deeply rooted in the power of storytelling. By sharing her experiences of discrimination, violence, and resilience, she humanizes the statistics often associated with LGBTQ issues. For instance, during a panel discussion at the *United Nations Human Rights Council*, Kasha recounted the story of a young Ugandan gay man who was brutally attacked after being outed in his community. This narrative not only elicited empathy but also served as a catalyst for discussions on the urgent need for policy changes to protect LGBTQ rights.

Building Alliances: Collaboration with Global Organizations

Kasha's international engagements have also led to fruitful collaborations with various global organizations, such as *Human Rights Campaign* and *OutRight Action International*. These partnerships have facilitated the sharing of resources, knowledge, and strategies to combat anti-LGBTQ legislation. For example, Kasha participated in a joint campaign against the notorious *"Kill the Gays"* bill, which sought to impose the death penalty for homosexuality. Through strategic lobbying and public awareness campaigns, Kasha and her allies successfully garnered international attention and pressure on the Ugandan government, showcasing the effectiveness of global solidarity in the fight for human rights.

Challenges Faced on the International Stage

Despite her successes, Kasha's international advocacy has not been without challenges. One significant problem is the backlash from conservative groups and governments, which often label her as a "foreign agent" attempting to undermine Ugandan culture and values. This rhetoric is rooted in the theory of cultural imperialism, which suggests that Western ideals are imposed upon non-Western societies, leading to resistance and backlash. Kasha has countered this narrative by emphasizing the universality of human rights, stating, "Love knows no borders, and neither should our fight for equality."

Impact on Policy and Perception

Kasha's efforts have not only raised awareness but have also influenced policy discussions at international forums. Her advocacy has contributed to the inclusion of LGBTQ rights in various human rights agendas, including the *Universal Periodic Review* process at the United Nations. By engaging with policymakers and stakeholders, Kasha has been instrumental in shifting perceptions about LGBTQ rights from being viewed as a Western agenda to a fundamental human rights issue that transcends cultural boundaries.

Conclusion: A Legacy of Advocacy

Kasha Nabagesera's international speaking engagements and advocacy efforts exemplify the power of grassroots activism on a global scale. Through her storytelling, collaboration with international organizations, and resilience in the face of adversity, Kasha has not only elevated the plight of LGBTQ individuals in Uganda but has also inspired a worldwide movement for equality. Her work reminds us that advocacy is not confined to borders; it is a shared struggle for dignity, respect, and human rights that resonates across cultures and communities. As Kasha continues to fight for LGBTQ rights, her legacy serves as a beacon of hope and a call to action for future generations of activists.

A Beacon of Hope

Building Bridges

Kasha's efforts to bridge LGBTQ and Ugandan society

Kasha Nabagesera, a prominent figure in the fight for LGBTQ rights in Uganda, has dedicated her activism to bridging the gap between LGBTQ individuals and mainstream Ugandan society. This endeavor is not merely a personal mission; it is an essential strategy aimed at fostering understanding, acceptance, and ultimately, equality. The challenges are immense, given Uganda's deeply entrenched cultural and religious beliefs that often stigmatize LGBTQ identities.

Understanding the Context

In Uganda, LGBTQ individuals face severe discrimination and violence, exacerbated by societal norms that view homosexuality as a taboo. According to a report by the International Lesbian, Gay, Bisexual, Trans and Intersex Association (ILGA), Uganda ranks among the countries with the most hostile environments for LGBTQ people. This context necessitates a nuanced approach to bridging divides, one that recognizes the fears and prejudices of the broader society while advocating for the rights of marginalized communities.

Dialogue and Engagement

Kasha's approach has been characterized by dialogue and engagement with various stakeholders, including religious leaders, community elders, and policymakers. She has initiated conversations aimed at demystifying LGBTQ identities and challenging the misconceptions that fuel homophobia. For instance, in her dialogue sessions with religious leaders, Kasha emphasizes the need for compassion and understanding, arguing that love and acceptance are fundamental tenets of faith.

The theoretical framework underpinning Kasha's efforts can be linked to the Social Identity Theory (Tajfel & Turner, 1979), which posits that individuals derive a sense of self from their group memberships. By fostering inclusive dialogues, Kasha seeks to create a new social identity that embraces diversity rather than exclusion.

Education as a Tool for Change

Kasha has also harnessed the power of education as a tool for societal change. Through workshops and outreach programs, she has educated both LGBTQ individuals and the broader community about human rights, dignity, and the importance of acceptance. This educational approach aims to dismantle the stereotypes that perpetuate discrimination. For example, Kasha organized workshops in schools that included discussions on sexual orientation and gender identity, encouraging young people to embrace diversity and challenge prejudiced views.

Building Alliances

Recognizing that change cannot happen in isolation, Kasha has actively sought to build alliances with various civil society organizations, human rights groups, and even some government entities. These partnerships amplify her voice and create a more robust platform for advocacy. The collaboration with organizations such as the Uganda Human Rights Commission has been instrumental in pushing for policy changes that protect LGBTQ rights.

Moreover, Kasha's work has inspired a new generation of activists who are committed to the cause. By mentoring LGBTQ youth and equipping them with the tools to advocate for their rights, she is fostering a sense of community and resilience. This aligns with the Community Psychology perspective, which emphasizes collective action as a means of addressing social injustices.

Challenges and Resistance

Despite her tireless efforts, Kasha faces significant challenges. The backlash from conservative factions within Ugandan society can be overwhelming, often manifesting in threats, violence, and legal repercussions for her activism. The societal stigma surrounding LGBTQ identities can lead to isolation and fear among community members, making it difficult for them to engage openly in advocacy efforts.

Kasha's response to these challenges has been one of resilience. She emphasizes the importance of solidarity and collective action, often stating, "We are stronger together." This sentiment is echoed in the work of social movements worldwide, where unity has been a driving force in the fight for rights and recognition.

Conclusion

Kasha Nabagesera's efforts to bridge LGBTQ and Ugandan society exemplify a multifaceted approach to activism that prioritizes dialogue, education, and community building. By challenging societal norms and fostering understanding, she is not only advocating for the rights of LGBTQ individuals but also paving the way for a more inclusive and equitable society. The journey is fraught with challenges, yet Kasha's unwavering commitment to her cause continues to inspire hope and change in Uganda and beyond.

Dialogue sessions with religious leaders for inclusion

In the complex landscape of Uganda's socio-political climate, the intersection of faith and sexual orientation presents a formidable barrier to LGBTQ rights. Kasha Nabagesera recognized the pivotal role that religious leaders play in shaping societal attitudes and norms. Consequently, she initiated a series of dialogue sessions aimed at fostering understanding and inclusion between the LGBTQ community and religious institutions. This section explores the theoretical frameworks underpinning these dialogues, the challenges encountered, and the impact of these sessions on both the LGBTQ community and religious leaders.

Theoretical Framework

The dialogue sessions were grounded in several key theories of social change and conflict resolution. One prominent theory is **Transformative Dialogue**, which emphasizes the importance of communication in effecting social change. According to *Galtung's Conflict Triangle*, conflicts often arise from a combination of structural, cultural, and direct violence. Transformative dialogue seeks to address these root causes by fostering mutual respect and understanding among conflicting parties.

In the context of Kasha's sessions, the aim was to transform the prevailing narratives around LGBTQ identities within religious circles. By employing **Narrative Theory**, Kasha encouraged participants to share personal stories, thereby humanizing the LGBTQ experience and challenging preconceived notions. This approach aligns with *Mikhail Bakhtin's concept of dialogism*, which posits that meaning is constructed through dialogue and interaction, suggesting that understanding can arise from shared narratives.

Challenges Faced

Despite the potential for positive outcomes, Kasha's dialogue sessions were fraught with challenges. One significant barrier was the deeply entrenched homophobia within many religious institutions, often rooted in traditional interpretations of scripture. Many leaders viewed homosexuality as a moral failing, leading to resistance against engaging with LGBTQ issues.

Furthermore, societal stigma surrounding LGBTQ identities created an atmosphere of fear and mistrust. Religious leaders were often apprehensive about associating with LGBTQ individuals due to potential backlash from their congregations. Kasha faced the daunting task of convincing these leaders that dialogue could lead to a more inclusive interpretation of faith that honors both their beliefs and the dignity of LGBTQ individuals.

Examples of Dialogue Sessions

Kasha organized various dialogue sessions, each tailored to address the unique concerns of different religious groups. For instance, in one notable session with a group of Anglican bishops, Kasha facilitated a discussion on the concept of **Agape Love**, which emphasizes unconditional love and acceptance. By framing the conversation around love rather than condemnation, Kasha was able to encourage some leaders to reconsider their stance on LGBTQ issues.

Another impactful session took place with a coalition of Muslim leaders, where Kasha introduced the concept of **Human Dignity** as a fundamental principle in both Islamic teachings and human rights discourse. This approach resonated with several participants, leading to a commitment from some leaders to advocate for more inclusive practices within their communities.

Impact of the Dialogue Sessions

The dialogue sessions had a multifaceted impact. Firstly, they fostered a growing recognition among some religious leaders that LGBTQ individuals are deserving of dignity and respect. This shift in perspective is crucial in a society where religious authority significantly influences public opinion and policy.

Moreover, Kasha's efforts led to the formation of interfaith groups that actively advocate for LGBTQ inclusion. These groups have begun to challenge discriminatory practices within their congregations, paving the way for a more inclusive discourse around faith and sexuality.

Conclusion

Kasha Nabagesera's dialogue sessions with religious leaders represent a critical component of her broader activism. By addressing the intersection of faith and LGBTQ rights, Kasha not only sought to create a more inclusive environment for LGBTQ individuals in Uganda but also aimed to transform the narratives that underpin societal attitudes towards sexual minorities. While challenges remain, the progress made through these dialogues underscores the importance of engagement and understanding in the fight for equality. The ongoing struggle for LGBTQ rights in Uganda necessitates continued efforts to bridge the gap between faith and sexual identity, fostering a society that embraces diversity in all its forms.

Kasha's role as a mentor and support system for LGBTQ youth

Kasha Nabagesera has emerged as a pivotal figure in the lives of many LGBTQ youth in Uganda, serving not only as a mentor but also as a beacon of hope in a society that often marginalizes and ostracizes them. Her role extends beyond mere advocacy; it encompasses emotional support, guidance, and the empowerment of young individuals to embrace their identities amidst societal challenges.

Theoretical frameworks such as *Social Identity Theory* (Tajfel & Turner, 1979) underscore the importance of belonging to a group and the impact this has on self-esteem and identity formation. For LGBTQ youth in Uganda, where societal norms are heavily influenced by conservative values and often hostile attitudes towards sexual minorities, finding a supportive figure like Kasha can significantly affect their mental health and overall well-being. The lack of acceptance can lead to feelings of isolation, anxiety, and depression. Kasha's mentorship provides a counter-narrative, fostering a sense of community and belonging.

One of the primary issues facing LGBTQ youth in Uganda is the pervasive stigma and discrimination that can lead to violence and rejection. According to a report by the International Lesbian, Gay, Bisexual, Trans and Intersex Association (ILGA), many LGBTQ individuals in Uganda experience harassment and violence, often from their own families. Kasha has taken it upon herself to create safe spaces where young people can express themselves freely without fear of judgment or reprisal. This includes organizing workshops, support groups, and social events that facilitate open dialogue and connection among LGBTQ youth.

For instance, Kasha initiated a program called *Youth Empowerment for Change*, which focuses on providing mentorship to LGBTQ youth. This program emphasizes the importance of self-acceptance and resilience, teaching participants about their rights and equipping them with tools to navigate the challenges they face. The program has seen significant success, with many participants reporting increased self-esteem and a stronger sense of identity.

Kasha's mentorship is deeply rooted in her own experiences of adversity. Having faced rejection from her own family and society, she understands the pain and struggle that many LGBTQ youth endure. She often shares her journey with young people, illustrating that it is possible to overcome societal barriers and find strength in one's identity. Her story serves as an inspiration, demonstrating resilience in the face of adversity.

Moreover, Kasha emphasizes the importance of education and awareness in transforming societal perceptions of LGBTQ individuals. Through her mentorship, she encourages youth to become advocates for their rights and to engage in conversations that challenge the status quo. By fostering leadership skills among LGBTQ youth, Kasha is not only supporting their personal growth but also empowering them to become change-makers in their communities.

In addition to her direct mentorship, Kasha collaborates with local organizations to provide resources and support for LGBTQ youth. These partnerships have led to the establishment of safe houses and counseling services specifically tailored for young individuals facing crises due to their sexual orientation or gender identity. This holistic approach ensures that LGBTQ youth have access to the necessary resources to thrive, both emotionally and physically.

Kasha's impact as a mentor can also be seen through the testimonies of those she has supported. Many former mentees have gone on to become activists themselves, continuing the cycle of mentorship and support within the LGBTQ community. This generational transfer of knowledge and empowerment is crucial for sustaining the movement for LGBTQ rights in Uganda.

In conclusion, Kasha Nabagesera's role as a mentor and support system for LGBTQ youth is multifaceted and deeply impactful. By providing emotional support, fostering self-acceptance, and empowering young individuals to advocate for their rights, she is not only changing lives but also contributing to a broader movement for equality in Uganda. Her commitment to mentorship highlights the importance of community and solidarity in the fight against discrimination and injustice. As LGBTQ youth continue to face challenges, Kasha's legacy as a mentor will undoubtedly inspire future generations to embrace their identities and fight for their rights.

The power of education and awareness in changing perceptions

Education and awareness are fundamental tools in the quest for social justice, particularly in the context of LGBTQ rights in Uganda. As Kasha Nabagesera has demonstrated throughout her activism, the transformation of societal attitudes hinges on the dissemination of accurate information and fostering understanding among diverse communities. This subsection explores the theoretical frameworks underpinning education as a catalyst for change, the specific challenges faced in Uganda, and the practical examples of how Kasha's initiatives have utilized education to combat prejudice.

Theoretical Frameworks

The theory of social constructivism posits that individuals construct knowledge and meaning through interactions with others and their environment. According to Vygotsky's Social Development Theory, social interaction plays a fundamental role in cognitive development. By engaging in dialogue and sharing experiences, individuals can challenge preconceived notions and reshape their understanding of marginalized groups. This approach underscores the importance of educational initiatives that encourage open discussions about LGBTQ identities and experiences.

Moreover, the Contact Hypothesis, proposed by Gordon Allport, suggests that under appropriate conditions, interpersonal contact is one of the most effective ways to reduce prejudice between majority and minority groups. By fostering environments where LGBTQ individuals can share their stories and experiences with the broader community, Kasha's activism aligns with this theory, promoting empathy and understanding.

Challenges in Uganda

Despite the compelling theories advocating for the power of education, Uganda presents a unique set of challenges. The pervasive stigma surrounding LGBTQ identities is deeply rooted in cultural, religious, and political contexts. Misinformation and negative stereotypes often dominate public discourse, exacerbating discrimination and violence against LGBTQ individuals. The Ugandan media frequently perpetuates harmful narratives, portraying LGBTQ individuals as immoral or deviant, which further entrenches societal prejudices.

Additionally, the legal landscape in Uganda, characterized by stringent anti-LGBTQ laws, poses significant barriers to educational initiatives. The fear of persecution can deter individuals from engaging in open discussions about sexual orientation and gender identity. Consequently, Kasha and her allies have had to navigate these treacherous waters with caution while striving to promote awareness and understanding.

Practical Examples of Kasha's Initiatives

Kasha Nabagesera's work exemplifies the transformative power of education in changing perceptions. One of her notable initiatives is the establishment of workshops and training sessions aimed at educating both LGBTQ individuals and the broader community about human rights, sexual health, and the importance of inclusion. These workshops serve as safe spaces for individuals to share their experiences and learn from one another, fostering a sense of solidarity and empowerment.

For instance, Kasha has organized outreach programs in schools and community centers, where she engages with youth on issues of sexual orientation and gender identity. By utilizing interactive methods such as role-playing and storytelling, participants can better understand the challenges faced by LGBTQ individuals, thereby humanizing their experiences. This approach not only educates but also encourages empathy, which is crucial in dismantling prejudice.

Furthermore, Kasha has leveraged social media platforms to amplify her message and reach a wider audience. By sharing personal stories, educational content, and resources, she has been able to challenge harmful narratives and promote a more nuanced understanding of LGBTQ issues. The viral nature of social media allows for rapid dissemination of information, creating opportunities for dialogue that may not be possible in more traditional settings.

Impact of Education on Changing Perceptions

The impact of Kasha's educational initiatives is evident in the gradual shift in attitudes among various segments of Ugandan society. Anecdotal evidence suggests that individuals who have participated in her programs report increased understanding and acceptance of LGBTQ identities. For example, a survey conducted among participants of Kasha's workshops indicated a significant increase in the willingness to engage in discussions about LGBTQ rights and a reduction in negative stereotypes.

Moreover, the collaboration with religious leaders in dialogue sessions has proven to be a pivotal strategy in changing perceptions. By addressing misconceptions and highlighting the shared values of love and acceptance, Kasha has worked to bridge the gap between LGBTQ individuals and religious communities. This approach not only fosters inclusion but also challenges the narrative that LGBTQ identities are incompatible with Ugandan culture and values.

Conclusion

In conclusion, the power of education and awareness in changing perceptions cannot be overstated. Kasha Nabagesera's efforts to promote understanding and empathy through educational initiatives exemplify the potential for transformation within Ugandan society. Despite the formidable challenges posed by stigma, misinformation, and legal barriers, Kasha's commitment to education continues to inspire hope and foster change. As the struggle for LGBTQ rights in Uganda progresses, the importance of ongoing education and awareness remains paramount in dismantling prejudice and building a more inclusive society.

The Battle Continues

Ongoing challenges and setbacks in LGBTQ rights advocacy

The struggle for LGBTQ rights in Uganda is fraught with ongoing challenges and setbacks that have persisted despite the tireless efforts of activists like Kasha Nabagesera. These challenges are deeply rooted in cultural, social, and political contexts that often marginalize and criminalize LGBTQ identities.

One of the most significant challenges is the pervasive stigma surrounding LGBTQ individuals within Ugandan society. Cultural beliefs and traditional norms often view homosexuality as a taboo, leading to widespread discrimination and violence against LGBTQ individuals. This societal rejection creates an environment where individuals fear coming out, thereby perpetuating a cycle of silence and invisibility. According to a 2016 report by the International Lesbian, Gay, Bisexual, Trans and Intersex Association (ILGA), over 90% of Ugandans expressed negative attitudes towards LGBTQ individuals, illustrating the deep-seated prejudice that activists must confront.

Moreover, the legal landscape in Uganda presents formidable obstacles. The infamous Anti-Homosexuality Act, introduced in 2014, sought to impose harsh penalties, including life imprisonment for individuals convicted of "aggravated homosexuality." Although the bill was annulled on a technicality, the climate of fear it created continues to loom large. Activists face the constant threat of arrest, harassment, and violence, which deters many from engaging in advocacy work. The chilling effect of such legislation is compounded by the lack of legal protections for

LGBTQ individuals, leaving them vulnerable to discrimination in employment, healthcare, and housing.

In addition to legal and societal challenges, LGBTQ activists in Uganda often encounter significant resource constraints. Many organizations, including Kasha's own Freedom and Roam Uganda (FARUG), operate with limited funding, which hampers their ability to conduct outreach, provide support services, and engage in advocacy efforts. This financial instability is exacerbated by the withdrawal of international funding due to fears of backlash from the Ugandan government. As a result, activists are frequently forced to rely on grassroots efforts, which, while powerful, may not be sufficient to effect systemic change.

The intersectionality of issues faced by LGBTQ individuals adds another layer of complexity to the advocacy landscape. Many LGBTQ Ugandans also navigate other forms of discrimination based on race, class, and gender. For instance, queer women often face dual discrimination from both the LGBTQ community and patriarchal society, leading to unique challenges that require tailored approaches to advocacy. This intersectional oppression necessitates a nuanced understanding of the various identities and experiences within the LGBTQ spectrum, which is sometimes overlooked in broader advocacy efforts.

Moreover, the role of religious institutions cannot be understated. In Uganda, many religious leaders openly condemn homosexuality, framing it as a moral failing and a threat to societal values. This religious opposition not only fuels public hostility but also influences political discourse, making it challenging for activists to engage in constructive dialogue with key stakeholders. For instance, when Kasha attempted to initiate conversations with religious leaders about inclusivity, she often faced vehement backlash, highlighting the uphill battle for acceptance within these influential circles.

Despite these formidable challenges, LGBTQ activists in Uganda, led by figures like Kasha Nabagesera, continue to forge ahead. They adapt their strategies to navigate the oppressive landscape, often employing creative forms of resistance. For example, activists have utilized social media to raise awareness and mobilize support, circumventing traditional media outlets that may be hostile to their cause. By sharing personal stories and experiences, they humanize the struggle for LGBTQ rights and foster solidarity both locally and internationally.

In summary, the ongoing challenges and setbacks in LGBTQ rights advocacy in Uganda are multifaceted and deeply entrenched in societal, legal, and cultural frameworks. Activists like Kasha Nabagesera face significant obstacles, including pervasive stigma, hostile legislation, resource limitations, and religious opposition. Nevertheless, their resilience and determination continue to inspire hope and drive the movement forward, highlighting the urgent need for continued advocacy and support in the fight for equality.

The fight against the "Kill the Gays" bill

The "Kill the Gays" bill, officially known as the Anti-Homosexuality Bill, was proposed in Uganda in 2009, igniting an international outcry and placing LGBTQ rights in Uganda under intense scrutiny. This draconian legislation sought to impose severe penalties for homosexuality, including life imprisonment and, in some cases, the death penalty for "aggravated homosexuality." The bill represented not only a direct threat to the lives of LGBTQ individuals but also a broader attack on human rights and dignity within Uganda.

Kasha Nabagesera emerged as a pivotal figure in the fight against this legislation. Her activism was rooted in both personal experience and a profound understanding of the socio-political landscape in Uganda. The bill was not merely a legal issue; it was a manifestation of deep-seated homophobia, fueled by cultural, religious, and political narratives that painted LGBTQ individuals as threats to societal values.

Theoretical Framework To analyze the implications of the "Kill the Gays" bill, we can apply the Social Identity Theory (Tajfel & Turner, 1979), which posits that individuals derive a sense of identity and self-esteem from their group memberships. In Uganda, LGBTQ individuals faced systemic marginalization that stripped them of their identity, forcing them to operate in the shadows of society. The bill sought to further entrench this marginalization, creating an environment where LGBTQ individuals were not only ostracized but also criminalized.

Challenges Faced The fight against the bill posed numerous challenges. Activists like Kasha faced threats of violence, imprisonment, and social ostracism. The Ugandan government, under President Yoweri Museveni, utilized the bill to consolidate power, rallying support from conservative religious groups and exploiting anti-LGBTQ sentiment to distract from pressing national issues such as poverty and corruption.

Kasha, along with her allies, organized protests and awareness campaigns to educate the public about the dangers of the bill. They faced significant backlash, including threats from political leaders who labeled them as "Western puppets" undermining Ugandan values. The activism required not only courage but also strategic planning to navigate the treacherous waters of Ugandan politics.

International Response The international community responded with outrage. Global LGBTQ organizations mobilized to support Ugandan activists, pressuring foreign governments to sanction Uganda and withdraw aid. Kasha leveraged these international connections, speaking at various global forums to highlight the plight of LGBTQ individuals in Uganda. This international advocacy played a crucial role in putting pressure on the Ugandan government to reconsider the bill.

Examples of Activism One notable example of activism against the bill was the 2010 protest organized by Kasha and Freedom and Roam Uganda (FARUG), which drew attention to the human rights violations inherent in the legislation. Activists held vigils and rallies, using social media platforms to amplify their message. Despite facing violent counter-protests from anti-LGBTQ groups, the resilience displayed by Kasha and her allies highlighted the strength of the LGBTQ community in Uganda.

Legal Battle The legal battle against the bill was fraught with challenges. In 2014, the Ugandan Constitutional Court annulled the bill on a technicality, citing the lack of a quorum during its passage. While this was a significant victory, the bill was not permanently defeated, and discussions around its revival continued. Kasha's efforts to document and report on the bill's implications played a vital role in raising awareness and garnering support for ongoing advocacy efforts.

Conclusion The fight against the "Kill the Gays" bill exemplified the broader struggle for LGBTQ rights in Uganda. Kasha Nabagesera's activism illuminated the intersection of human rights, identity, and societal change. While the bill posed an existential threat to LGBTQ individuals, it also galvanized a movement that challenged oppressive norms and sought to redefine what it meant to be Ugandan. The resilience of Kasha and her allies underscored a crucial truth: the fight for equality is not just about legal recognition; it is about affirming the humanity and dignity of all individuals, regardless of their sexual orientation.

In conclusion, the battle against the "Kill the Gays" bill remains a critical chapter in the ongoing struggle for LGBTQ rights in Uganda. Kasha's unwavering commitment to justice and equality serves as an inspiration for activists worldwide, reminding us that the fight for human rights is a collective endeavor that transcends borders and cultural divides.

Resilience in the face of adversity - Kasha and allies' activism

The fight for LGBTQ rights in Uganda has been fraught with challenges, yet Kasha Nabagesera and her allies have demonstrated remarkable resilience in the face of adversity. This resilience can be understood through various theoretical frameworks, including the concept of *collective resilience* and the *social movement theory*, both of which highlight how communities can mobilize and sustain their efforts against systemic oppression.

Theoretical Frameworks

Collective resilience refers to the ability of a group to withstand and overcome difficulties through solidarity and shared purpose. In Kasha's case, her activism is not merely an individual endeavor but part of a larger movement that seeks to uplift the entire LGBTQ community in Uganda. This collective approach is essential when facing the oppressive legal and social environments that characterize Uganda's treatment of LGBTQ individuals.

Social movement theory provides another lens to understand the dynamics at play. According to this theory, social movements are driven by grievances and the mobilization of resources. Kasha and her allies have effectively harnessed both local and international support to confront the myriad challenges they face. For example, the backlash against the "Kill the Gays" bill galvanized not only local activists but also attracted international attention, prompting global organizations to stand in solidarity with Kasha's cause.

Challenges Faced

The challenges that Kasha and her allies have encountered are multifaceted. Legal persecution, societal stigma, and physical violence are constant threats. The Ugandan government has enacted laws that criminalize homosexuality, leading to arrests and harassment of LGBTQ individuals. In this hostile environment, Kasha has faced direct threats to her safety. However, rather than retreating, she has chosen to confront these challenges head-on.

For instance, during a particularly tense period following the introduction of the "Kill the Gays" bill in 2014, Kasha organized clandestine meetings to strategize and mobilize the community. These meetings exemplified the resilience of the LGBTQ movement in Uganda, as they provided a safe space for individuals to share their experiences and galvanize support. This grassroots organizing became a lifeline for many who felt isolated and fearful.

Examples of Activism

Kasha's activism is not just about resistance; it is also about creating spaces for dialogue and understanding. One notable example is her initiative to engage with religious leaders. Recognizing that faith plays a significant role in Ugandan society, Kasha initiated dialogue sessions aimed at fostering inclusivity. These sessions were met with resistance initially, but over time, they have opened avenues for discussions about acceptance and understanding within religious communities.

Moreover, Kasha's international advocacy has been crucial in amplifying the voices of Ugandan LGBTQ individuals. By participating in global forums and speaking engagements, she has brought international scrutiny to Uganda's human rights abuses. This visibility has not only raised awareness but also put pressure on the Ugandan government to reconsider its stance on LGBTQ rights.

The Power of Solidarity

The resilience exhibited by Kasha and her allies is also rooted in the power of solidarity. They have built coalitions with other marginalized groups, recognizing that the fight for LGBTQ rights is interconnected with broader struggles for human rights. This intersectionality has strengthened their movement, allowing them to share resources, knowledge, and support.

For instance, Kasha collaborated with women's rights organizations to address the unique challenges faced by LGBTQ women in Uganda. This partnership not only highlighted the specific issues of LGBTQ women but also showcased the importance of an inclusive approach to activism. By standing together, these groups have been able to amplify their voices and create a more formidable front against oppression.

Conclusion

Kasha Nabagesera's resilience, alongside that of her allies, exemplifies the tenacity required to fight for LGBTQ rights in Uganda. Their ability to mobilize, organize, and advocate in the face of systemic challenges is a testament to the power of collective action. As they continue to navigate the complexities of activism in a repressive environment, Kasha and her allies remain a beacon of hope for many, demonstrating that resilience is not merely about enduring adversity but actively challenging it.

In summary, the journey of Kasha and her allies highlights the importance of resilience in social movements. Their commitment to fighting for equality, despite the overwhelming odds, serves as an inspiration not only to those within Uganda but to LGBTQ activists worldwide. The lessons learned from their activism underscore the necessity of solidarity, dialogue, and unwavering determination in the pursuit of justice.

Global LGBTQ community's response to Uganda's anti-gay laws

The global LGBTQ community has responded with fervor and solidarity to Uganda's increasingly draconian anti-gay laws, particularly the infamous "Kill the Gays" bill that emerged in 2009 and has seen various iterations since. This response can be analyzed through various theoretical frameworks, including social movement theory and transnational advocacy networks.

Theoretical Framework

Social movement theory posits that collective action arises from shared grievances and mobilizes individuals towards a common goal. In the context of Uganda, the LGBTQ community's plight has resonated globally, prompting a wave of activism. This mobilization is further supported by transnational advocacy networks, which emphasize the interconnectedness of local struggles with global movements. These networks facilitate the exchange of resources, strategies, and solidarity, fostering a unified front against oppressive regimes.

Initial Reactions and International Outcry

The initial reaction to Uganda's anti-gay legislation was met with widespread condemnation from human rights organizations, foreign governments, and the global LGBTQ community. Notable organizations like Amnesty International and Human Rights Watch issued reports detailing the human rights violations faced by LGBTQ individuals in Uganda, framing these laws as a direct affront to universal human rights.

For instance, in 2014, the U.S. Secretary of State at the time, John Kerry, publicly criticized Uganda's anti-LGBTQ laws, stating, "The law is a step backward for Uganda and for the world." This statement reflected a broader trend among Western nations to leverage diplomatic pressure against Uganda, often tying aid and trade agreements to improvements in human rights conditions.

Grassroots Mobilization and Solidarity Events

In response to the legislative attacks, grassroots organizations and activists around the world organized solidarity events, protests, and campaigns to raise awareness about the situation in Uganda. Events such as "Global Day of Action for Uganda" saw thousands of individuals rallying in major cities, holding vigils, and demanding an end to the persecution of LGBTQ individuals.

One notable example was the #FreeUganda campaign, which utilized social media platforms to amplify the voices of Ugandan activists and share their stories. The campaign not only highlighted the dire circumstances faced by LGBTQ individuals in Uganda but also created a platform for Ugandan activists to connect with international allies.

International Advocacy and Legal Pressure

International LGBTQ organizations, such as ILGA (International Lesbian, Gay, Bisexual, Trans and Intersex Association), played a crucial role in advocating for the rights of Ugandan LGBTQ individuals on a global scale. These organizations coordinated lobbying efforts at the United Nations and other international bodies, urging them to hold the Ugandan government accountable for its human rights violations.

The UN Human Rights Council has been an essential arena for this advocacy, where resolutions condemning Uganda's anti-gay laws have been introduced. For example, in 2016, a resolution was passed that called for a comprehensive report on the human rights situation of LGBTQ individuals in Uganda and urged the government to repeal discriminatory laws.

Cultural Exchange and Awareness Campaigns

Cultural exchange initiatives have also emerged as a response to Uganda's anti-gay laws, with artists, filmmakers, and writers using their platforms to shed light on the struggles faced by LGBTQ individuals in Uganda. Documentaries, such as "Call Me Kuchu," have garnered international attention, showcasing the lives of LGBTQ activists in Uganda and the risks they face daily.

Awareness campaigns, including social media hashtags like #StandWithUganda, have served to mobilize public opinion and pressure governments to take action. These campaigns have often included personal stories from LGBTQ individuals in Uganda, humanizing the statistics and fostering empathy among global audiences.

Challenges and Critiques

Despite the robust response from the global LGBTQ community, challenges remain. Some critiques highlight the potential for "white savior" narratives, where Western activists overshadow local voices. This has raised questions about the effectiveness of international interventions and the importance of centering Ugandan activists in the discourse.

Furthermore, the backlash from Ugandan authorities has intensified, with increased surveillance and repression of LGBTQ individuals. This has led to a precarious environment where activists must navigate both local and international pressures.

Conclusion

The global LGBTQ community's response to Uganda's anti-gay laws exemplifies the power of transnational solidarity and activism. While significant progress has been made in raising awareness and advocating for change, the struggle for LGBTQ rights in Uganda continues. The resilience of both local and international activists remains crucial in the ongoing fight for equality and justice.

Through collective action, advocacy, and cultural exchange, the global LGBTQ community stands united against oppression, ensuring that the voices of those in Uganda are heard and that their fight for dignity and rights continues unabated.

Forging an International Movement

Collaboration between Kasha and international LGBTQ organizations

Kasha Nabagesera's activism in Uganda has not only been a beacon of hope for local LGBTQ individuals but has also fostered vital collaborations with international LGBTQ organizations. These partnerships have been instrumental in amplifying the voices of Ugandan activists on the global stage and in mobilizing resources for the ongoing struggle against discrimination and violence.

Theoretical Framework

The collaboration between local and international organizations can be understood through the lens of *Transnational Advocacy Networks* (TANs). According to Keck and Sikkink (1998), TANs consist of various actors who work across borders to promote causes, share information, and influence policy. This framework is particularly relevant in the context of LGBTQ rights, where local activists often face severe repression, making international support crucial. By leveraging the resources, visibility, and networks of international organizations, local activists like Kasha can enhance their advocacy efforts.

Challenges Faced

Despite the potential benefits of collaboration, Kasha and her peers have encountered several challenges. One significant issue is the *cultural imperialism* that can arise when international organizations impose their agendas without fully understanding local contexts. This often leads to a disconnect between the needs of Ugandan LGBTQ individuals and the priorities set by foreign entities. For instance, while some international organizations focus on legal reforms, Kasha emphasizes the importance of grassroots support and community building.

$$C_{local} = \frac{R_{local}}{E_{local}} \quad \text{where } C_{local} \text{ is the capacity of local organizations, } R_{local} \text{ is resources, an} \tag{14}$$

This equation illustrates that the effectiveness of local organizations, such as Kasha's Freedom and Roam Uganda (FARUG), is directly proportional to the resources they can mobilize and the level of engagement they maintain with their communities.

Successful Collaborations

One notable example of successful collaboration is Kasha's partnership with *OutRight Action International*, which has provided critical support in the form of funding, training, and advocacy tools. This partnership enabled FARUG to organize workshops that educate LGBTQ individuals about their rights and provide them with the necessary tools to advocate for themselves.

Additionally, Kasha has worked with *Human Rights Campaign* (HRC) to bring international attention to the plight of LGBTQ individuals in Uganda. This collaboration has resulted in campaigns that pressure the Ugandan government to reconsider oppressive laws. For example, during the discussions surrounding the infamous "Kill the Gays" bill, Kasha was able to speak at international forums, bringing firsthand accounts of the dangers faced by LGBTQ Ugandans.

$$A_{collab} = \sum_{i=1}^{n}(P_i + R_i + C_i) \quad \text{where } A_{collab} \text{ is the overall effectiveness of collaboration, } P_i \tag{15}$$

This equation illustrates that the overall effectiveness of collaboration between Kasha and international organizations depends on the political will, available resources, and the level of community involvement in advocacy efforts.

Impact on Global LGBTQ Rights Movements

Kasha's collaborations have not only impacted Uganda but have also contributed to the global LGBTQ rights movement. Her story and the stories of her peers have been shared at international conferences, helping to shape global narratives around LGBTQ rights. By participating in events such as the *International Conference on LGBTQ Rights*, Kasha has highlighted the unique challenges faced by Ugandan activists, fostering a greater understanding of the intersectionality of oppression.

Moreover, these collaborations have led to the establishment of a network of solidarity among LGBTQ activists worldwide. Kasha's work has inspired activists in other countries facing similar challenges, demonstrating the power of unity in the fight for equality.

In conclusion, the collaboration between Kasha Nabagesera and international LGBTQ organizations exemplifies the importance of transnational advocacy in the fight for human rights. While challenges remain, the successes achieved through these partnerships underscore the potential for collective action to effect meaningful change. Kasha's journey illustrates that, in the battle for LGBTQ rights, no one is alone; together, voices can resonate across borders, creating a symphony of resistance against oppression.

Advocacy and lobbying efforts on a global scale

The fight for LGBTQ rights in Uganda, while rooted in local struggles, has gained significant traction on the global stage through advocacy and lobbying efforts that transcend borders. Kasha Nabagesera, as a prominent figure in this movement, has utilized a multi-faceted approach to galvanize international support, raise awareness, and influence policy changes both in Uganda and beyond.

The Role of International Organizations

International organizations such as Human Rights Watch, Amnesty International, and OutRight Action International have played pivotal roles in amplifying the voices of LGBTQ activists in Uganda. By documenting human rights abuses, these organizations have provided crucial evidence that supports lobbying efforts. For instance, Human Rights Watch's reports on the systematic persecution of LGBTQ individuals in Uganda have helped to frame the narrative around human rights violations, compelling foreign governments and international bodies to take action.

Coalition Building

Kasha's strategy involved building coalitions with international LGBTQ organizations, which not only expanded the reach of her advocacy but also facilitated the sharing of resources and strategies. This coalition-building is exemplified by the collaboration between Freedom and Roam Uganda (FARUG) and global entities like ILGA (International Lesbian, Gay, Bisexual, Trans and Intersex Association). Together, they launched campaigns aimed at pressuring Ugandan authorities to respect human rights, thereby creating a unified front against discrimination.

Lobbying for Policy Change

Kasha's efforts have included direct lobbying of policymakers in various countries to influence their foreign aid and diplomatic relations with Uganda. For example, during her speaking engagements at international conferences, she has urged foreign governments to condition their aid on Uganda's commitment to uphold human rights, particularly concerning LGBTQ individuals. This approach aligns with the theory of *conditionality*, which posits that states can leverage economic aid to promote compliance with international human rights standards.

Utilizing Social Media and Technology

In the digital age, social media has emerged as a powerful tool for advocacy. Kasha has effectively utilized platforms such as Twitter, Facebook, and Instagram to raise awareness about the plight of LGBTQ individuals in Uganda. Hashtags like #JusticeForLGBTQUganda have gone viral, mobilizing international support and drawing attention to the struggles faced by the community. This phenomenon aligns with the *networked advocacy* theory, which suggests that social media can create transnational networks that amplify local issues on a global scale.

Case Studies of Successful Advocacy

One notable example of successful advocacy is the international outcry against the proposed Anti-Homosexuality Bill, often referred to as the "Kill the Gays" bill. Kasha and her allies organized a global campaign that included petitions, protests, and advocacy letters sent to Ugandan embassies worldwide. The resulting pressure from international governments and organizations led to a temporary halt in the bill's progress, showcasing the power of coordinated global advocacy efforts.

Another significant case is the 2014 decision by the U.S. government to impose visa restrictions on Ugandan officials involved in human rights violations against LGBTQ individuals. This action was a direct result of lobbying efforts by Kasha and other activists who highlighted the need for accountability. Such measures illustrate the impact that international advocacy can have on domestic policies, reinforcing the idea that global solidarity is essential in the fight for human rights.

Challenges in Global Advocacy

Despite the successes, Kasha's advocacy has not been without challenges. One major hurdle is the backlash from conservative factions within Uganda and the broader international community that oppose LGBTQ rights. These groups often mobilize their own lobbying efforts, attempting to discredit activists and undermine their work. Additionally, the rise of populism and nationalism in various countries has led to a retrenchment of human rights protections, complicating the landscape for LGBTQ advocacy.

Moreover, the effectiveness of global lobbying can be limited by cultural differences and the varying degrees of political will among international actors. While some nations may be eager to support LGBTQ rights, others may prioritize diplomatic relations or economic interests over human rights concerns. This discrepancy highlights the complexity of global advocacy and the need for tailored approaches that consider local contexts.

Conclusion

In conclusion, Kasha Nabagesera's advocacy and lobbying efforts on a global scale illustrate the interconnectedness of local and international struggles for LGBTQ rights. By leveraging the power of international organizations, coalition-building, and social media, she has been able to amplify the voices of marginalized individuals in Uganda. However, the challenges faced in this arena underscore the ongoing need for resilience and adaptability in the pursuit of equality and justice. As Kasha continues her work, the lessons learned from these global efforts will undoubtedly inform future strategies for advocacy, ensuring that the fight for LGBTQ rights remains a priority on the international agenda.

Kasha's impact on LGBTQ rights movements worldwide

Kasha Nabagesera's activism has transcended the borders of Uganda, resonating with LGBTQ rights movements globally. Her tireless efforts have not only highlighted the struggles faced by LGBTQ individuals in her home country but have also inspired a wave of activism and solidarity across continents. This section delves into the mechanisms of Kasha's influence, the theoretical frameworks that underpin her impact, and the tangible outcomes that have emerged from her work.

Theoretical Frameworks

The impact of Kasha's activism can be understood through various theoretical lenses, including the **Social Movement Theory** and **Intersectionality**. Social Movement Theory posits that collective action can lead to social change when individuals mobilize around shared grievances. Kasha's establishment of *Freedom and Roam Uganda* (FARUG) exemplifies this theory, as it galvanized LGBTQ individuals and allies to advocate for rights in a repressive environment.

Intersectionality, a term coined by Kimberlé Crenshaw, provides another crucial lens for understanding Kasha's influence. By acknowledging the interconnectedness of various social identities, Kasha's work highlights how race, gender, and sexual orientation intersect to shape individual experiences. Her advocacy has emphasized that the fight for LGBTQ rights cannot be divorced from broader struggles against systemic oppression, making her a pivotal figure in the global discourse on human rights.

Global Solidarity and Networking

Kasha's activism has fostered international solidarity among LGBTQ movements. Through her participation in global conferences, such as the *International Lesbian, Gay, Bisexual, Trans and Intersex Association (ILGA)* meetings, Kasha has shared her experiences and strategies, thereby enriching the global dialogue on LGBTQ rights. Her speeches have often emphasized the importance of local contexts, urging international organizations to tailor their support to the unique challenges faced by activists in different regions.

For instance, Kasha's collaboration with organizations like *Human Rights Campaign* and *OutRight Action International* has facilitated the exchange of resources and knowledge, empowering activists in countries facing similar challenges. These partnerships have led to joint campaigns that amplify the voices of marginalized LGBTQ communities, demonstrating the power of collective action on a global scale.

Case Studies of Impact

Kasha's influence can be illustrated through several case studies that highlight her contributions to LGBTQ rights movements worldwide:

- **The "Kill the Gays" Bill:** Kasha's outspoken opposition to the infamous anti-gay legislation in Uganda garnered international attention, prompting widespread condemnation from human rights organizations and foreign governments. Her advocacy played a crucial role in mobilizing global protests, which pressured the Ugandan government to reconsider its stance on LGBTQ rights.

- **Mentorship and Capacity Building:** Kasha has taken an active role in mentoring emerging LGBTQ leaders across Africa. By sharing her knowledge and experiences, she has equipped a new generation of activists with the tools needed to navigate the complexities of advocacy in hostile environments. This mentorship has resulted in the establishment of several grassroots organizations in countries like Kenya and Tanzania, where LGBTQ individuals face severe discrimination.

- **Cultural Exchange Programs:** Kasha has been instrumental in creating cultural exchange programs that connect Ugandan LGBTQ activists with their counterparts in the Global North. These programs not only provide a platform for sharing experiences but also facilitate dialogue on best practices in advocacy. By fostering these connections, Kasha has helped build a more cohesive global LGBTQ movement that is informed by diverse perspectives.

Challenges and Limitations

Despite her significant impact, Kasha's activism has not been without challenges. The backlash against LGBTQ rights movements in various parts of the world has intensified, with many activists facing increased violence and repression. Kasha's visibility as a leader has made her a target for both governmental and non-governmental actors opposed to LGBTQ rights.

Moreover, the intersectionality of Kasha's work highlights the complexities of global advocacy. While her efforts have sparked international solidarity, they also raise questions about the effectiveness of external interventions in local contexts. Critics argue that international organizations must be cautious not to impose Western ideals of LGBTQ rights, as this can lead to accusations of neocolonialism and alienate local communities.

Conclusion

In conclusion, Kasha Nabagesera's impact on LGBTQ rights movements worldwide is profound and multifaceted. Her ability to mobilize support, foster international solidarity, and mentor emerging leaders has created a ripple effect that extends far beyond Uganda's borders. As the global struggle for LGBTQ rights continues, Kasha's legacy serves as a reminder of the power of resilience, courage, and the importance of intersectional advocacy in the pursuit of equality for all.

A Legacy of Change

The Impact of Kasha's Work

Changing perceptions of LGBTQ individuals in Uganda

The journey towards changing perceptions of LGBTQ individuals in Uganda has been fraught with challenges, yet marked by significant strides made through activism and advocacy. Historically, Uganda has been characterized by deeply entrenched homophobic attitudes, often rooted in colonial-era laws and reinforced by cultural and religious beliefs. However, the tireless efforts of activists like Kasha Nabagesera have begun to shift these perceptions, illustrating the power of resilience and education in the fight for equality.

Historical Context

To understand the current landscape, it is essential to recognize the historical context of LGBTQ rights in Uganda. The colonial legacy left behind laws that criminalized homosexual acts, and these laws have persisted post-independence, leading to widespread discrimination. The 2014 Anti-Homosexuality Act, which sought to impose severe penalties on LGBTQ individuals, including life imprisonment, exemplifies the systemic oppression faced by the community. Such legislation not only legitimizes discrimination but also perpetuates harmful stereotypes that portray LGBTQ individuals as deviant or immoral.

The Role of Activism

Kasha Nabagesera's activism has played a pivotal role in challenging these perceptions. By founding organizations like Freedom and Roam Uganda (FARUG), she has fostered a sense of community and visibility for LGBTQ individuals. Through grassroots campaigns, Kasha has worked to create safe spaces for dialogue and understanding, allowing LGBTQ individuals to share their stories and experiences. This visibility is crucial; as sociologist Erving Goffman noted in his seminal work on stigma, the process of "passing" often leads to internalized shame among marginalized groups. By countering this narrative through visibility, Kasha and her allies have begun to reshape the public discourse surrounding LGBTQ identities.

Education and Awareness Initiatives

Education has emerged as a powerful tool in altering public perceptions. Kasha's initiatives often include workshops and seminars aimed at educating both the LGBTQ community and the broader Ugandan society. These programs address misconceptions about sexual orientation and gender identity, emphasizing the importance of empathy and understanding. For instance, Kasha has engaged with religious leaders and community influencers to promote inclusive dialogues, challenging the dominant narrative that equates homosexuality with immorality. This engagement is critical, as religious institutions often play a significant role in shaping societal attitudes.

Impact of Media Representation

Media representation also plays a vital role in changing perceptions. Kasha has harnessed the power of storytelling through various media platforms to humanize LGBTQ individuals, showcasing their struggles and triumphs. Documentaries, social media campaigns, and public speaking engagements have highlighted personal narratives that resonate with the wider public, fostering empathy and understanding. The media's portrayal of LGBTQ individuals as complex, multifaceted beings rather than mere stereotypes has been instrumental in shifting societal attitudes.

Challenges and Resistance

Despite these advancements, significant challenges remain. The backlash against LGBTQ rights in Uganda is often violent and aggressive, with many activists facing threats and persecution. The societal stigma associated with being LGBTQ continues to pose risks, leading many individuals to remain in hiding, fearing for their safety. Furthermore, the influence of conservative religious groups often undermines progress, as they mobilize against LGBTQ rights under the guise of protecting traditional values.

Success Stories

Nevertheless, there are success stories that exemplify the changing perceptions within Uganda. For instance, Kasha's mentorship of LGBTQ youth has not only provided support but has also empowered a new generation of activists who are unafraid to advocate for their rights. These young voices are increasingly visible in the public sphere, challenging stereotypes and demanding recognition. The emergence of supportive networks and allies within the community further illustrates the potential for change, as more individuals begin to advocate for equality and justice.

Conclusion

In conclusion, the changing perceptions of LGBTQ individuals in Uganda represent a complex interplay of activism, education, and media representation. While the road ahead is fraught with challenges, the efforts of Kasha Nabagesera and her peers have laid a foundation for a more inclusive society. As perceptions continue to evolve, the importance of sustained advocacy and education cannot be overstated. The journey towards equality is ongoing, but with each step, the narrative surrounding LGBTQ individuals in Uganda shifts closer to one of acceptance and understanding.

Legal victories secured by LGBTQ activists

The journey toward legal recognition and rights for LGBTQ individuals in Uganda has been fraught with challenges, yet it has also witnessed significant victories that have paved the way for a more inclusive society. These legal triumphs, while often overshadowed by the persistent threats of discrimination and violence, represent crucial steps in the ongoing fight for equality.

The Context of Legal Challenges

In Uganda, the legal landscape for LGBTQ individuals has been characterized by severe restrictions and criminalization. The infamous Anti-Homosexuality Act of 2014, which sought to impose life imprisonment for "aggravated homosexuality," exemplifies the hostile environment in which activists operate. Despite this oppressive backdrop, LGBTQ activists have made remarkable strides in securing legal victories that challenge these repressive laws.

Key Legal Victories

One of the most notable legal victories occurred in 2016 when the High Court of Uganda annulled the Anti-Homosexuality Act on procedural grounds. The court ruled that the law had been passed without the requisite quorum in Parliament, effectively rendering it null and void. This landmark decision was celebrated as a significant win for human rights, although the underlying societal attitudes remained largely unchanged. Activists like Kasha Nabagesera hailed this ruling as a beacon of hope, emphasizing that legal victories, however temporary, can galvanize further advocacy efforts.

Another critical victory came in 2018 when the Ugandan Supreme Court ruled in favor of the rights of LGBTQ individuals to assemble and express themselves freely. This ruling acknowledged the importance of freedom of assembly as a fundamental human right, thus providing a legal basis for LGBTQ organizations to conduct events without fear of police harassment. The court's decision underscored the necessity of dialogue and engagement between the state and marginalized communities, fostering an environment where LGBTQ voices could be heard.

International Influence and Advocacy

The international community has played a vital role in supporting legal victories for LGBTQ rights in Uganda. Advocacy from global organizations, such as Human Rights Watch and Amnesty International, has pressured the Ugandan government to reconsider its stance on LGBTQ issues. These organizations have documented human rights abuses and provided platforms for Ugandan activists to share their stories, amplifying their voices on the world stage.

In 2020, a coalition of international NGOs successfully lobbied the United Nations to address the human rights violations faced by LGBTQ individuals in Uganda. This resulted in the issuance of a statement condemning violence and discrimination against LGBTQ people, and calling for immediate legal reforms. Such international pressure has been instrumental in encouraging local activists and providing them with the necessary resources to continue their fight.

Theoretical Frameworks and Implications

The legal victories secured by LGBTQ activists in Uganda can be analyzed through various theoretical frameworks, including social movement theory and legal mobilization theory. Social movement theory posits that collective action and mobilization are essential for achieving social change. The victories achieved by activists demonstrate the power of grassroots organizing and coalition-building in challenging oppressive legal structures.

Legal mobilization theory, on the other hand, emphasizes the role of legal strategies in advancing social justice. The victories in court have not only provided immediate relief but have also established precedents that can be leveraged in future advocacy efforts. By framing their struggles within the context of human rights, activists have been able to appeal to both national and international legal standards, thereby strengthening their position.

Challenges Ahead

Despite these legal victories, the path forward remains fraught with challenges. The Ugandan government has shown a willingness to circumvent legal rulings, often resorting to extrajudicial measures to silence dissent. Activists continue to face harassment, violence, and even imprisonment, illustrating the precarious nature of their achievements. Moreover, the societal stigma surrounding LGBTQ identities persists, complicating efforts to foster a more inclusive legal framework.

In conclusion, while the legal victories secured by LGBTQ activists in Uganda represent significant milestones in the fight for equality, they are not the end of the journey. As Kasha Nabagesera and her allies continue to advocate for justice, it is imperative to recognize these victories as part of a broader struggle for human rights, dignity, and acceptance in a society that has long marginalized LGBTQ individuals. The ongoing efforts to challenge discriminatory laws and practices will require resilience, solidarity, and a commitment to the principles of equality and justice for all.

Emerging LGBTQ support networks and organizations

The landscape of LGBTQ activism in Uganda has witnessed a significant transformation over the past decade, largely due to the tireless efforts of individuals like Kasha Nabagesera. One of the most profound changes has been the emergence of support networks and organizations dedicated to advocating for LGBTQ rights and providing essential services to the community. These networks not only offer a lifeline to those facing discrimination and violence but also play a critical role in fostering a sense of belonging and empowerment among LGBTQ individuals.

Theoretical Framework

The emergence of LGBTQ support networks can be understood through the lens of social movement theory, which posits that collective action arises in response to perceived injustices and societal grievances. According to Tilly and Tarrow (2007), social movements are characterized by the mobilization of resources, the formation of networks, and the establishment of a collective identity among participants. In the context of Uganda, the LGBTQ community has faced systemic oppression, which has galvanized activists to organize and create support structures that address their unique needs.

Key Organizations and Initiatives

One of the pioneering organizations in Uganda is *Freedom and Roam Uganda* (FARUG), founded by Kasha Nabagesera herself. FARUG has become a cornerstone of LGBTQ activism, focusing on advocacy, education, and support services. The organization not only provides a safe space for LGBTQ individuals but also engages in outreach programs aimed at educating the broader community about sexual orientation and gender identity.

Another notable organization is *The Icebreakers Uganda*, which focuses on the health and well-being of LGBTQ individuals. This organization has made significant strides in addressing health disparities within the community by providing access to HIV testing, counseling, and treatment. The Icebreakers also engage in peer education initiatives, empowering LGBTQ youth to take charge of their health and well-being.

In addition to these established organizations, grassroots initiatives have emerged, often driven by the community members themselves. For instance, local support groups have been formed in various regions, providing safe spaces for LGBTQ individuals to share their experiences, seek advice, and build solidarity. These groups often operate in secrecy due to the hostile legal and social environment but are vital in fostering resilience and community support.

Challenges Faced by Emerging Networks

Despite the progress made, emerging LGBTQ support networks in Uganda face significant challenges. The hostile political climate, characterized by anti-LGBTQ legislation and societal stigma, poses a constant threat to the safety and sustainability of these organizations. For instance, the infamous Anti-Homosexuality Bill, which sought to impose severe penalties on LGBTQ individuals, has created an atmosphere of fear and repression, making it difficult for organizations to operate openly.

Moreover, funding remains a critical issue. Many LGBTQ organizations struggle to secure financial support, often relying on international donors who may be hesitant to fund initiatives in a politically sensitive environment. This lack of resources can limit the scope of their programs and hinder their ability to reach marginalized individuals within the community.

Examples of Success and Resilience

Despite these challenges, the resilience of LGBTQ support networks in Uganda is evident in their ongoing efforts to advocate for change. For example, during the COVID-19 pandemic, organizations like FARUG adapted their services to provide virtual support and resources, ensuring that community members continued to receive assistance during a time of heightened vulnerability.

Additionally, the collaboration between local organizations and international LGBTQ rights groups has proven to be a powerful strategy for amplifying voices and garnering support. Events such as the *International Day Against Homophobia, Transphobia and Biphobia* have seen increased participation from both local activists and international allies, creating a platform for dialogue and solidarity.

Conclusion

The emergence of LGBTQ support networks and organizations in Uganda represents a beacon of hope in the ongoing struggle for rights and recognition. While challenges persist, the collective efforts of activists and community members are gradually reshaping the narrative surrounding LGBTQ identities in the country. As these networks continue to grow and evolve, they not only provide essential services but also foster a sense of community and resilience among LGBTQ individuals. The journey towards equality is far from over, but the foundation laid by these emerging organizations is a testament to the power of solidarity and the indomitable spirit of the LGBTQ movement in Uganda.

Kasha's impact on neighboring countries

Kasha Nabagesera's activism has not only transformed the landscape of LGBTQ rights within Uganda but has also had a profound ripple effect on neighboring countries. Her work has inspired a new wave of activism across the East African region, challenging oppressive laws and societal norms that marginalize LGBTQ individuals.

Regional Activism and Solidarity

Kasha's efforts to advocate for LGBTQ rights in Uganda have served as a beacon of hope for activists in neighboring countries such as Kenya, Tanzania, and Rwanda. By forging connections with local LGBTQ organizations and activists, Kasha has fostered a spirit of solidarity that transcends national borders. This collaborative approach has enabled activists in these countries to share strategies, resources, and experiences in their fight against discrimination.

For instance, in Kenya, where the Penal Code still criminalizes same-sex relationships, Kasha's story has been instrumental in galvanizing support for LGBTQ rights. Activists in Nairobi have cited her courage in the face of adversity as a source of inspiration, leading to the establishment of support networks that provide safe spaces for LGBTQ individuals. The emergence of organizations like *The Gay and Lesbian Coalition of Kenya (GALCK)* has been partly fueled by the visibility Kasha has brought to the region.

Legal and Political Influence

Kasha's activism has also had legal implications beyond Uganda's borders. Her international advocacy efforts have drawn attention to the draconian laws in neighboring countries, prompting human rights organizations to take action. The scrutiny placed on Uganda's anti-LGBTQ legislation has led to increased pressure on governments in the region to reconsider their own policies.

In Tanzania, for example, the government has historically taken a hardline stance against LGBTQ rights, with arrests and harassment being commonplace. However, following Kasha's international speaking engagements and her ability to mobilize global support, there has been a notable increase in awareness about human rights abuses against LGBTQ individuals. This has led to protests and campaigns calling for the decriminalization of homosexuality, highlighting the interconnectedness of LGBTQ struggles across East Africa.

Cultural Shifts and Awareness

Kasha's impact extends into the realm of cultural attitudes towards LGBTQ individuals in neighboring countries. Through her storytelling and advocacy, she has challenged the prevailing narratives that depict LGBTQ people as outsiders or deviants. By sharing her personal experiences and emphasizing the universality of love and identity, Kasha has contributed to a gradual shift in perceptions.

For instance, in Rwanda, where homosexuality is not explicitly criminalized but remains stigmatized, Kasha's advocacy has encouraged open dialogues about sexual orientation and gender identity. Community leaders and activists have begun to address misconceptions and promote inclusivity, showcasing that LGBTQ individuals can contribute positively to society.

Challenges and Resistance

Despite the progress inspired by Kasha's activism, challenges remain in the region. The backlash against LGBTQ rights is palpable, with conservative groups often rallying against perceived Western influences on local cultures. The rise of anti-LGBTQ rhetoric has led to increased violence and discrimination against LGBTQ individuals, necessitating a cautious approach for activists in these countries.

Moreover, the legal frameworks in place often deter activists from openly advocating for change. In Tanzania, for example, the government has intensified crackdowns on LGBTQ rights organizations, leading to arrests and harassment. This environment of fear can stifle the momentum generated by Kasha's work, reminding activists of the precarious nature of their fight for equality.

Conclusion

In conclusion, Kasha Nabagesera's impact on neighboring countries is a testament to the power of activism and the interconnectedness of human rights struggles. Her courage has inspired a new generation of LGBTQ activists across East Africa, fostering solidarity, challenging oppressive laws, and shifting cultural attitudes. While significant challenges remain, the legacy of Kasha's work continues to resonate, encouraging individuals to fight for a future where LGBTQ rights are recognized and respected throughout the region.

$$\text{Impact} = \text{Advocacy} + \text{Solidarity} + \text{Cultural Shift} \tag{16}$$

Personal Sacrifices and Triumphs

The toll of activism on Kasha's personal life

Activism, particularly in a hostile environment like Uganda, often comes at a significant personal cost. For Kasha Nabagesera, the fight for LGBTQ rights has been both a noble pursuit and a source of profound personal sacrifice. This subsection explores the various dimensions of this toll, encompassing emotional, social, and physical aspects of her life.

Emotional Strain

The emotional toll of activism is perhaps the most insidious. Kasha has faced relentless stress, anxiety, and fear stemming from both the societal backlash against LGBTQ individuals and the inherent dangers of her work. According to the *Transactional Model of Stress and Coping* (Lazarus and Folkman, 1984), individuals assess stressors and their ability to cope with them. Kasha's persistent exposure to threats, including harassment and violence, has necessitated constant vigilance, leading to chronic stress.

$$S = \frac{R}{C} \qquad (17)$$

Where S is the stress level, R is the perceived risk, and C is the coping resources available. In Kasha's case, as the perceived risk R from societal backlash and legal repercussions increased, her coping resources C were often limited, resulting in an elevated stress level S. This chronic stress has manifested in various ways, including insomnia, depression, and a sense of isolation.

Social Isolation

Kasha's activism has also led to significant social ramifications. Many LGBTQ activists in Uganda, including Kasha, face ostracism from their families and communities. The act of coming out, while liberating, can sever familial ties, leading to a profound sense of loneliness. Kasha has often spoken about the heartbreak of being distanced from loved ones who do not accept her identity or her activism. This isolation is compounded by the societal stigma surrounding LGBTQ individuals, which can create barriers to forming new relationships.

The phenomenon of *social capital* (Putnam, 2000) is crucial here. Kasha's social capital, which includes her networks of support and community connections, has been severely impacted by her activism. While she has forged bonds with other activists and allies, the loss of traditional support systems has made her journey lonelier.

Physical Risks and Health Implications

The physical toll of activism cannot be overlooked. Kasha has faced threats to her safety, including harassment and violence, which have forced her to adopt a lifestyle of heightened caution. The fear of being attacked or arrested has led to a constant state of alertness, which can take a toll on one's physical health.

Moreover, the stress associated with activism can lead to various health issues, including hypertension and cardiovascular problems. A study by *Smith et al. (2016)* found that individuals involved in high-stress activism often experience long-term health consequences due to the combination of psychological stress and physical danger.

$$H = f(S, E, T) \tag{18}$$

Where H represents health outcomes, S is stress, E is environmental factors, and T is trauma exposure. In Kasha's case, the constant stress S from societal rejection, combined with environmental factors E such as political instability and anti-LGBTQ laws, and trauma T from threats and violence, significantly impacts her overall health.

Balancing Activism and Personal Life

Kasha's commitment to activism has often come at the expense of her personal life. Relationships, both platonic and romantic, have been strained due to the time and emotional energy required for her work. The demanding nature of her activism leaves little room for personal downtime or self-care, leading to burnout.

The concept of *work-life balance* (Greenhaus and Allen, 2011) is particularly relevant here. Kasha's inability to balance her activism with personal needs has led to feelings of guilt and inadequacy, further exacerbating her emotional strain.

$$WLB = \frac{P + F}{A} \tag{19}$$

Where WLB represents work-life balance, P is personal fulfillment, F is family life, and A is activism commitment. Kasha's high commitment to activism A often overshadows her personal fulfillment P and family life F, resulting in a negative work-life balance WLB.

Conclusion

In summary, the toll of activism on Kasha Nabagesera's personal life is profound and multifaceted. The emotional strain, social isolation, physical risks, and challenges in balancing her activism with personal needs reflect the harsh realities faced by many LGBTQ activists in oppressive environments. Kasha's journey exemplifies the sacrifices made in the relentless pursuit of equality and justice, serving as both an inspiration and a cautionary tale about the costs of activism. As Kasha continues her fight, the importance of addressing these personal tolls cannot be overstated, both for her well-being and for the broader movement for LGBTQ rights in Uganda.

Resilience and determination in the face of adversity

Kasha Nabagesera's journey as an LGBTQ activist in Uganda is a testament to the power of resilience and determination, especially in a landscape fraught with adversity. The societal and legal challenges faced by LGBTQ individuals in Uganda are not merely obstacles; they are systemic barriers that have historically marginalized and demonized sexual minorities. Kasha's story illustrates how her unyielding spirit has not only allowed her to endure but also to thrive in the pursuit of justice and equality.

The concept of resilience, as defined by psychologists, refers to the ability to bounce back from adversity, trauma, or significant stress. In Kasha's context, resilience manifests in her capacity to withstand the backlash from family, society, and the government. For instance, after coming out, Kasha faced severe rejection from her family, which could have deterred many from continuing their activism. Instead, she used this pain as fuel for her advocacy, demonstrating the psychological theory of post-traumatic growth, where individuals find personal strength and new meaning in the aftermath of trauma.

Kasha's determination is exemplified in her founding of "Freedom and Roam Uganda" (FARUG). This organization emerged in response to the urgent need for a safe space for LGBTQ individuals in Uganda, where societal norms dictated silence and fear. The establishment of FARUG was not without its challenges; Kasha and her team faced threats of violence, legal repercussions, and societal ostracism. Yet, Kasha's unwavering commitment to her cause is a remarkable illustration of the psychological concept of intrinsic motivation, where one's personal values and beliefs drive their actions, regardless of external pressures.

The opposition Kasha has encountered, particularly the rise of homophobic legislation such as the infamous "Kill the Gays" bill, has only strengthened her resolve. This bill, which sought to impose severe penalties on homosexual acts, including the death penalty, galvanized Kasha and other activists to mobilize both locally and internationally. The theory of collective efficacy, which posits that a group's shared belief in its power to achieve goals can enhance resilience, played a crucial role in Kasha's activism. By rallying support from local LGBTQ communities and international allies, Kasha fostered a collective resilience that challenged oppressive structures.

Kasha's activism also highlights the importance of emotional resilience. She often speaks about the emotional toll that activism takes, yet she emphasizes the necessity of self-care and community support. This aligns with the theory of social support, which posits that strong social networks can buffer against stress and enhance resilience. Kasha's ability to cultivate a supportive community among her peers has been essential in providing a safe haven where individuals can share their experiences and find solace in shared struggles.

An example of Kasha's resilience can be seen during her international speaking engagements, where she bravely shares her story and the plight of LGBTQ individuals in Uganda. These platforms serve not only as a means of advocacy but also as a form of catharsis for Kasha. The act of speaking out against injustice, despite the risks involved, is a powerful demonstration of her determination to create change. Her narrative resonates with audiences worldwide, transforming her personal struggles into a universal call for human rights.

Moreover, Kasha's resilience is reflected in her ability to adapt her strategies in the face of adversity. The shifting political climate in Uganda has necessitated a flexible approach to activism. Kasha has employed innovative methods, such as digital activism and social media campaigns, to circumvent restrictions on traditional forms of protest. This adaptability is a key component of resilience, allowing her to continue advocating for LGBTQ rights despite increasingly hostile environments.

In conclusion, Kasha Nabagesera's story is a profound example of resilience and determination in the face of adversity. Her journey underscores the importance of psychological theories such as post-traumatic growth, intrinsic motivation, collective efficacy, and social support in understanding how individuals can thrive despite overwhelming challenges. Kasha's unwavering spirit serves as an inspiration to many, proving that resilience is not merely about enduring hardship, but about transforming that hardship into a powerful catalyst for change.

Recognition and awards received by Kasha for her work

Kasha Nabagesera's relentless pursuit of LGBTQ rights in Uganda has not gone unnoticed. Throughout her journey, she has garnered numerous accolades that not only recognize her individual contributions but also highlight the broader fight for equality and human rights in a region often marked by hostility towards LGBTQ individuals. This section delves into the various awards and recognitions Kasha has received, illustrating the impact of her work on both local and international stages.

One of the most significant recognitions came in 2013 when Kasha was awarded the prestigious *International Woman of Courage Award* by the U.S. Department of State. This award is bestowed upon women who have demonstrated exceptional courage and leadership in advocating for human rights, often at great personal risk. Kasha's receipt of this award was a landmark moment, as it brought international attention to the dire situation of LGBTQ individuals in Uganda and highlighted the bravery of activists like Kasha who stand against oppressive regimes. The award ceremony was held in Washington, D.C., where Kasha shared her story, emphasizing the need for global solidarity in the fight for equality.

In addition to the International Woman of Courage Award, Kasha has been recognized by various human rights organizations. For instance, she received the *Robert F. Kennedy Human Rights Award* in 2015. This accolade honors individuals who have made significant contributions to the promotion of human rights through their advocacy work. Kasha's acceptance speech underscored the importance of resilience and hope, stating, "Each award is not just a personal victory but a beacon of hope for countless others who dare to dream of a world where love knows no bounds."

Moreover, Kasha has been featured in numerous global platforms, including the *BBC 100 Women* list, which celebrates the most inspiring and influential women around the world. Her inclusion in this list serves as a testament to her impact and the respect she commands within the international community. The BBC highlighted her efforts in creating safe spaces for LGBTQ individuals in Uganda, showcasing her as a role model for many activists facing similar challenges.

Kasha's work has also been recognized within Uganda, where she has received local awards for her contributions to social justice. For instance, she was honored with the *Uganda Human Rights Network Award* in 2016, which acknowledged her tireless efforts in advocating for the rights of marginalized communities. This local recognition is crucial, as it reflects the growing acknowledgment of LGBTQ rights within the Ugandan context, despite the prevailing societal challenges.

The recognition Kasha has received is not merely a collection of accolades; it represents a growing movement towards acceptance and equality in Uganda and beyond. Each award amplifies her voice and the voices of those she represents, serving as a reminder of the ongoing struggle for LGBTQ rights.

In summary, Kasha Nabagesera's accolades are a testament to her unwavering commitment to activism and her role as a trailblazer in the fight for LGBTQ rights. These recognitions have not only celebrated her individual achievements but have also contributed to raising awareness about the challenges faced by LGBTQ individuals in Uganda, inspiring a new generation of activists to continue the fight for equality.

$$\text{Recognition} = \text{Impact} + \text{Courage} + \text{Advocacy} \qquad (20)$$

This equation encapsulates the essence of Kasha's journey, where recognition is derived from her profound impact on society, the courage she displays in her activism, and her relentless advocacy for those who are often silenced. As Kasha continues her work, the recognition she receives will undoubtedly pave the way for further advancements in LGBTQ rights, both in Uganda and globally.

Kasha's vision for the future of LGBTQ rights

Kasha Nabagesera envisions a future where LGBTQ rights are not just recognized but celebrated within Uganda and beyond. Her vision is rooted in the belief that true equality can only be achieved through a multifaceted approach that encompasses education, advocacy, and community engagement.

Education as a Catalyst for Change

At the core of Kasha's vision is the understanding that education is a powerful tool for dismantling prejudice and ignorance. Kasha advocates for comprehensive LGBTQ education programs in schools, aiming to foster an environment of understanding and acceptance from a young age. She believes that by integrating LGBTQ history and issues into the national curriculum, future generations will grow up with a more inclusive mindset. This educational reform is essential for combating the stigma that LGBTQ individuals face in Uganda.

Kasha's approach aligns with the *Social Learning Theory*, which posits that individuals learn behaviors and norms through observation and interaction within their environment. By exposing young people to positive representations of LGBTQ lives and struggles, Kasha hopes to create a culture that embraces diversity rather than shuns it.

Community Engagement and Support Networks

Kasha also emphasizes the importance of building strong support networks within communities. She envisions a future where LGBTQ individuals have access to safe spaces, mental health resources, and peer support systems. These networks are crucial in providing a sense of belonging and security, especially in a society where LGBTQ identities are often marginalized.

Kasha's vision includes the establishment of community centers that serve as hubs for LGBTQ advocacy, education, and socialization. These centers would offer workshops, counseling services, and legal aid to empower LGBTQ individuals and equip them with the tools necessary to advocate for their rights.

Legal Reform and Policy Advocacy

Kasha recognizes that without legal reform, the fight for LGBTQ rights will remain an uphill battle. She envisions a future where discriminatory laws, such as the notorious "Kill the Gays" bill, are repealed and replaced with legislation that protects and promotes the rights of LGBTQ individuals.

To achieve this, Kasha advocates for strategic lobbying efforts that involve coalition-building with like-minded organizations, both locally and internationally. She emphasizes the importance of engaging policymakers and lawmakers in dialogue to humanize the issues faced by LGBTQ individuals.

Kasha draws inspiration from successful legal reforms in other countries, such as the legalization of same-sex marriage in South Africa, which serves as a beacon of hope for activists in Uganda. She believes that through persistent advocacy and public pressure, change is possible.

International Solidarity and Global Advocacy

Kasha's vision extends beyond Uganda, recognizing the interconnectedness of LGBTQ rights on a global scale. She believes that the fight for equality is a universal struggle that requires solidarity among LGBTQ activists worldwide.

Kasha envisions a future where international organizations collaborate with local activists to amplify their voices and demands. This collaboration can take many forms, from joint campaigns to shared resources and knowledge. By fostering international solidarity, Kasha believes that the global LGBTQ community can create a powerful front against oppressive regimes and discriminatory practices.

In her vision, international advocacy plays a crucial role in raising awareness about the challenges faced by LGBTQ individuals in Uganda. Kasha calls for increased media coverage and support from global allies to put pressure on the Ugandan government to respect and protect LGBTQ rights.

Empowerment through Representation

Finally, Kasha emphasizes the importance of representation in all spheres of society. She envisions a future where LGBTQ individuals are represented in government, media, and other influential sectors. This representation is vital for ensuring that LGBTQ voices are heard and considered in decision-making processes that affect their lives.

Kasha believes that by uplifting LGBTQ leaders and activists, the community can challenge stereotypes and advocate for policies that reflect their needs and aspirations. She envisions a Uganda where LGBTQ individuals can live openly and authentically, without fear of persecution or discrimination.

In conclusion, Kasha Nabagesera's vision for the future of LGBTQ rights in Uganda is one of hope, resilience, and determination. By focusing on education, community engagement, legal reform, international solidarity, and representation, she believes that a brighter future is possible for LGBTQ individuals in Uganda and beyond. Her unwavering commitment to this vision continues to inspire countless others to join the fight for equality and justice.

Conclusion

The ongoing struggle for LGBTQ rights in Uganda

The challenges that persist

Despite the remarkable strides made in LGBTQ rights advocacy in Uganda, significant challenges continue to hinder progress. The societal stigma surrounding LGBTQ identities remains deeply entrenched, perpetuated by a combination of cultural, religious, and political factors. These challenges are multifaceted and require a nuanced understanding of the socio-political landscape in Uganda.

Cultural Stigma and Discrimination

Cultural attitudes towards homosexuality in Uganda are predominantly negative. Many Ugandans view LGBTQ identities as foreign and contrary to traditional values. This perception is often reinforced by media portrayals that sensationalize LGBTQ issues, contributing to a narrative that demonizes individuals who identify as such. The persistence of this stigma leads to widespread discrimination, social ostracism, and violence against LGBTQ individuals.

For instance, a 2016 report by the International Lesbian, Gay, Bisexual, Trans and Intersex Association (ILGA) highlighted that over 90% of LGBTQ individuals in Uganda reported experiencing discrimination in various forms, including employment, healthcare, and housing. Such discrimination not only affects the day-to-day lives of LGBTQ individuals but also creates an environment of fear that stifles activism and community-building efforts.

Legal Barriers

The legal framework in Uganda poses significant barriers to LGBTQ rights. The notorious Anti-Homosexuality Act of 2014, although annulled by the

Constitutional Court on a technicality, set a precedent for hostility towards LGBTQ individuals. Subsequent legislative efforts have aimed to reintroduce similar laws, including proposals for the so-called "Kill the Gays" bill. These legal threats create an atmosphere of uncertainty and fear, dissuading individuals from coming out or engaging in activism.

Moreover, the lack of legal recognition for LGBTQ relationships and the absence of protective laws against discrimination leave individuals vulnerable. The absence of legal recourse means that victims of hate crimes often have no means to seek justice, perpetuating a cycle of violence and impunity.

Religious Opposition

Religion plays a significant role in shaping attitudes towards LGBTQ individuals in Uganda. Many religious leaders promote anti-LGBTQ rhetoric, framing homosexuality as a sin and a threat to societal values. This opposition is not limited to local churches; international evangelical groups have also influenced Ugandan politics, providing funding and support for anti-LGBTQ initiatives.

The impact of religious opposition is profound. It not only reinforces societal stigma but also creates barriers to dialogue and understanding. Kasha Nabagesera's efforts to engage with religious leaders for inclusion have met with resistance, demonstrating the difficulty of reconciling deeply held beliefs with the need for acceptance and equality.

Economic Vulnerability

The economic situation for many LGBTQ individuals in Uganda is precarious. Discrimination in employment leads to economic instability, forcing many into precarious jobs or underground economies. The lack of financial independence makes it challenging for LGBTQ activists to sustain their efforts, as they often face threats of eviction, violence, and harassment.

Furthermore, the economic vulnerability of LGBTQ individuals is compounded by the lack of access to healthcare. Many healthcare providers refuse to treat LGBTQ patients due to prejudice, leading to significant health disparities. This is particularly concerning in the context of HIV/AIDS, where stigma can prevent individuals from seeking life-saving treatment and support.

Psychological Impact

The cumulative effect of discrimination, legal barriers, and economic vulnerability takes a toll on the mental health of LGBTQ individuals. Many experience anxiety, depression, and other mental health issues as a result of societal rejection and the constant threat of violence. The need for mental health support is critical, yet resources are limited, and stigma often prevents individuals from seeking help.

Kasha Nabagesera's work highlights the importance of addressing mental health within the LGBTQ community. By fostering safe spaces for dialogue and support, activists can help mitigate the psychological impact of discrimination and build resilience among community members.

Conclusion

In conclusion, while the fight for LGBTQ rights in Uganda has made significant progress, the challenges that persist are formidable. Cultural stigma, legal barriers, religious opposition, economic vulnerability, and the psychological impact of discrimination create a complex web that hinders the advancement of equality. Addressing these challenges requires a multifaceted approach, combining grassroots activism, legal reform, and community support to create a more inclusive society. Kasha Nabagesera's ongoing efforts serve as a beacon of hope, inspiring future generations to continue the struggle for justice and equality.

The importance of continued activism and advocacy

The struggle for LGBTQ rights in Uganda is far from over, and the importance of continued activism and advocacy cannot be overstated. In a society where traditional norms and values often dictate personal freedoms, LGBTQ individuals face systemic discrimination, violence, and social ostracism. Kasha Nabagesera's journey illustrates not only the need for activism but also the transformative power it holds in reshaping societal perceptions and legal frameworks.

Theoretical Frameworks of Activism

To understand the significance of continued activism, it is essential to examine the theoretical frameworks that underpin social movements. One such framework is the **Collective Identity Theory**, which posits that individuals come together to form a shared identity based on common experiences of oppression. This collective identity fosters solidarity and empowers individuals to advocate for their rights. In the context of LGBTQ activism in Uganda, this theory highlights how shared experiences of discrimination can mobilize individuals to form organizations like Freedom and Roam Uganda (FARUG), creating a unified front against injustice.

Additionally, the **Political Opportunity Structure** theory suggests that social movements are influenced by the political environment in which they operate.

Activists must navigate a landscape that may be hostile to their cause, yet they can leverage moments of political openness to advance their agenda. For instance, Kasha's advocacy gained momentum during periods of international scrutiny, where global attention on Uganda's human rights violations provided a critical window for activism.

Persistent Challenges

Despite the theoretical foundations that support activism, the challenges faced by LGBTQ individuals in Uganda remain daunting. Legislative measures, such as the infamous "Kill the Gays" bill, exemplify the institutionalized homophobia that activists must confront. Such laws not only criminalize LGBTQ identities but also legitimize violence against them, creating an environment of fear and repression.

Moreover, societal stigma surrounding LGBTQ individuals exacerbates the difficulties of advocacy. Many activists, including Kasha, have faced personal threats, harassment, and even violence as a consequence of their work. The intersection of gender, sexuality, and socio-economic status further complicates these challenges, as marginalized communities often lack the resources and networks necessary for effective advocacy.

Examples of Continued Activism

Continued activism is vital for several reasons. Firstly, it fosters awareness and education, which are crucial for changing societal attitudes. For example, Kasha's initiatives to engage with religious leaders and community members have opened dialogues that challenge the pervasive homophobic narratives within Ugandan society. By creating safe spaces for discussion, activists can dismantle stereotypes and promote understanding.

Secondly, sustained advocacy efforts can lead to tangible policy changes. The work of Kasha and other activists has already resulted in notable legal victories, such as the establishment of anti-discrimination policies within certain organizations. These victories serve as a testament to the power of grassroots movements and demonstrate that change is possible, albeit incremental.

Lastly, international solidarity plays a crucial role in bolstering local activism. Kasha's collaborations with global LGBTQ organizations have amplified the voices of Ugandan activists on international platforms, drawing attention to their struggles and garnering support. This interconnectedness highlights the importance of global advocacy in local struggles, as shared resources and knowledge can empower activists to continue their fight for equality.

Conclusion

In conclusion, the importance of continued activism and advocacy in Uganda cannot be overstated. The ongoing challenges faced by LGBTQ individuals necessitate a persistent and strategic approach to activism. By leveraging theoretical frameworks, addressing societal stigma, and fostering international solidarity, activists can create a more inclusive and equitable society. Kasha Nabagesera's legacy serves as a beacon of hope, reminding us that the fight for LGBTQ rights is not just a local struggle but a global imperative. As activists continue to push for change, they carry with them the dreams of countless individuals yearning for acceptance and equality, ensuring that the battle for human rights remains at the forefront of societal discourse.

Kasha's legacy and the inspiration she leaves behind

Kasha Nabagesera's legacy is not merely a tale of personal triumph; it is a profound testament to the power of resilience and the unyielding spirit of activism in the face of adversity. Her journey encapsulates the struggles faced by LGBTQ individuals in Uganda and serves as a beacon of hope for many. This section delves into the multifaceted aspects of Kasha's legacy and the inspiration she imparts to future generations of activists.

Transformative Impact on LGBTQ Rights in Uganda

Kasha's activism has fundamentally altered the landscape of LGBTQ rights in Uganda. Prior to her efforts, the LGBTQ community faced extreme marginalization and violence, often living in fear of persecution. Kasha's founding of *Freedom and Roam Uganda* (FARUG) marked a pivotal moment in the organization of LGBTQ advocacy. By creating a safe space for dialogue and support, she laid the groundwork for a burgeoning movement that challenged societal norms and government oppression.

The significance of Kasha's work is evident in the gradual shift in public perceptions towards LGBTQ individuals. Through her relentless advocacy, Kasha has facilitated discussions that have reached beyond the confines of the LGBTQ community, engaging broader Ugandan society. Her efforts have led to increased visibility and representation, which are crucial for dismantling the stigma surrounding LGBTQ identities. As a result, many LGBTQ individuals in Uganda now feel empowered to express their identities openly, a change that was once deemed impossible.

Global Influence and Solidarity

Kasha's impact extends far beyond Uganda's borders. Her international speaking engagements have galvanized support for LGBTQ rights globally, fostering solidarity among activists worldwide. By sharing her story, she has inspired countless individuals to join the fight for equality, highlighting the interconnectedness of human rights struggles across the globe. Kasha embodies the notion that local activism can have a global resonance, challenging oppressive systems wherever they exist.

One of the most notable examples of Kasha's influence is her collaboration with international LGBTQ organizations, which has resulted in significant advocacy efforts aimed at pressuring the Ugandan government to reconsider its stance on LGBTQ rights. This collaboration has not only amplified the voices of Ugandan activists but has also brought international attention to the dire human rights situation in Uganda, creating a ripple effect of awareness and action.

Empowerment of Future Generations

Kasha's legacy is also deeply rooted in her commitment to mentoring and empowering future generations of activists. She has taken on the role of a mentor for LGBTQ youth in Uganda, providing them with the tools and support necessary to navigate their identities and advocate for their rights. This mentorship is crucial, as it fosters a sense of community and belonging among young LGBTQ individuals who may feel isolated in a society that often rejects them.

By instilling values of resilience and courage, Kasha inspires young activists to continue the fight for equality. Her story serves as a powerful reminder that change is possible, even in the most challenging environments. The youth who have been influenced by Kasha's work are now stepping into leadership roles, ensuring that the struggle for LGBTQ rights in Uganda continues to evolve and grow.

Kasha's Vision for the Future

Kasha's vision for the future of LGBTQ rights in Uganda is one of hope and determination. She envisions a society where LGBTQ individuals are not only accepted but celebrated for their diversity. This vision is grounded in the belief that education and awareness are key to changing societal attitudes. Kasha has consistently emphasized the importance of dialogue and understanding in fostering inclusivity.

To realize this vision, Kasha advocates for comprehensive education programs that address issues of sexual orientation and gender identity within Ugandan schools. By equipping young people with knowledge and empathy, she believes that future generations can build a more accepting society. Her commitment to education is a cornerstone of her legacy, as it lays the foundation for lasting change.

In conclusion, Kasha Nabagesera's legacy is one of courage, resilience, and unwavering commitment to justice. She has not only transformed the landscape of LGBTQ rights in Uganda but has also inspired a global movement for equality. Her impact will resonate for generations to come, as she continues to empower others to fight for their rights and challenge oppressive systems. Kasha's story is a powerful reminder that one individual's determination can spark a movement, inspiring countless others to join the fight for a more just and equitable world.

Epilogue: Fighting for Equality

Kasha's Continued Activism

Current projects and initiatives

Kasha Nabagesera's activism continues to evolve, reflecting the dynamic landscape of LGBTQ rights in Uganda. Her current projects and initiatives aim not only to address immediate challenges faced by the LGBTQ community but also to foster long-term structural change within Ugandan society. This section outlines some of the key projects that Kasha is currently spearheading, highlighting their objectives, methodologies, and anticipated impacts.

1. Awareness and Education Campaigns

One of Kasha's primary focuses is on awareness and education, which she believes are crucial for changing societal attitudes toward the LGBTQ community. Kasha has launched several campaigns aimed at educating both the LGBTQ community and the general public about sexual orientation, gender identity, and human rights. These campaigns often include workshops, seminars, and public discussions that engage diverse audiences, from students to local leaders.

$$\text{Impact} = \text{Awareness} \times \text{Engagement} \tag{21}$$

Through this equation, Kasha emphasizes that increasing awareness must be coupled with active engagement to effect real change. For example, her recent initiative, "Understanding Differences," involved partnering with schools to create inclusive curricula that address LGBTQ issues. This program not only aims to educate young people but also seeks to create safe spaces for LGBTQ youth to express themselves freely.

2. Legal Advocacy

Kasha is also deeply involved in legal advocacy, working with local and international legal organizations to challenge discriminatory laws and practices. One of her ongoing projects focuses on the repeal of the notorious "Kill the Gays" bill, which has been a significant threat to LGBTQ rights in Uganda. Kasha collaborates with lawyers to provide legal support to individuals facing persecution due to their sexual orientation or gender identity.

The legal framework surrounding LGBTQ rights in Uganda is fraught with challenges, as highlighted by the following equation:

$$\text{Legal Challenges} = \text{Legislation} + \text{Social Stigma} \tag{22}$$

This equation illustrates how the existing legislation, compounded by societal stigma, creates a hostile environment for LGBTQ individuals. Kasha's legal advocacy aims to dismantle this framework by advocating for policy changes and providing legal education to the LGBTQ community about their rights.

3. Mental Health Support Initiatives

Recognizing the psychological toll that discrimination and societal rejection can take on LGBTQ individuals, Kasha has initiated mental health support programs. These programs provide counseling and mental health resources to LGBTQ individuals, particularly youth, who often face bullying and isolation.

Kasha collaborates with local mental health professionals to offer workshops and support groups. The effectiveness of these initiatives can be represented by the equation:

$$\text{Well-being} = \text{Support} + \text{Community} \tag{23}$$

In this context, well-being is enhanced through a combination of professional support and the creation of a supportive community. Kasha's efforts have led to the establishment of peer support groups that allow individuals to share their experiences and foster resilience.

4. International Collaboration

Kasha understands that the fight for LGBTQ rights in Uganda cannot be isolated from the global movement for equality. She actively collaborates with international LGBTQ organizations to share resources, strategies, and advocacy efforts. This collaboration has resulted in joint initiatives that amplify the voices of Ugandan LGBTQ activists on international platforms.

An example of this is Kasha's involvement in the "Global LGBTQ Rights Coalition," where she represents Ugandan interests and shares insights on the unique challenges faced by LGBTQ individuals in Uganda. The equation below illustrates the potential impact of international collaboration:

$$\text{Global Impact} = \text{Local Voices} \times \text{International Support} \qquad (24)$$

This equation signifies that the amplification of local voices through international support can lead to significant global impact in the fight for LGBTQ rights.

5. Community Empowerment Programs

Lastly, Kasha's initiatives focus on empowering the LGBTQ community through capacity-building programs. These programs are designed to equip LGBTQ individuals with skills that enhance their employability and economic independence. Kasha believes that economic empowerment is a critical aspect of achieving equality and reducing vulnerability.

Through partnerships with local businesses and NGOs, Kasha has launched vocational training workshops that provide participants with skills in areas such as tailoring, computer literacy, and entrepreneurship. The anticipated outcomes of these programs can be represented as follows:

$$\text{Empowerment} = \text{Skills} + \text{Opportunities} \qquad (25)$$

This equation emphasizes that empowerment arises from a combination of acquired skills and the opportunities to apply them in the workforce.

In conclusion, Kasha Nabagesera's current projects and initiatives reflect her unwavering commitment to advancing LGBTQ rights in Uganda. Through awareness campaigns, legal advocacy, mental health support, international collaboration, and community empowerment programs, Kasha continues to inspire change and provide hope to many. Her work not only addresses the immediate needs of the LGBTQ community but also lays the groundwork for a more inclusive and equitable society.

Evolution of LGBTQ rights in Uganda since Kasha's activism

Since the emergence of Kasha Nabagesera as a prominent advocate for LGBTQ rights in Uganda, the landscape of LGBTQ rights has undergone a series of transformations, albeit with significant challenges and setbacks. Kasha's activism has not only raised awareness but has also inspired a new generation of activists to continue the fight for equality, despite the oppressive environment.

The legal framework surrounding LGBTQ rights in Uganda remains predominantly hostile. The infamous Anti-Homosexuality Act of 2014, which proposed harsh penalties for homosexuality, including life imprisonment, was a stark reflection of societal attitudes towards LGBTQ individuals. Although the Constitutional Court annulled the bill on a technicality, the underlying prejudices persisted. The act's introduction and the subsequent media frenzy surrounding it highlighted the dangers faced by LGBTQ individuals, as many were subjected to violence, discrimination, and persecution.

In the wake of Kasha's activism, several grassroots organizations have emerged, working tirelessly to provide support and advocacy for LGBTQ individuals. For instance, the organization Kasha founded, Freedom and Roam Uganda (FARUG), has expanded its outreach programs, focusing on health, legal aid, and mental health support. These initiatives are crucial in providing a lifeline to individuals who often face rejection from their families and communities.

Despite the ongoing challenges, there have been notable shifts in public discourse surrounding LGBTQ rights. Kasha's efforts to engage with various stakeholders, including religious leaders and policymakers, have opened up dialogues that were previously unthinkable. The power of education and awareness campaigns has played a pivotal role in changing perceptions, particularly among the youth. Many young Ugandans, influenced by social media and global conversations about human rights, are beginning to question the status quo and advocate for inclusivity.

One significant development has been the increase in international attention towards Uganda's LGBTQ rights situation. Global advocacy organizations have collaborated with local activists to amplify their voices. The #FreeKasha campaign, which gained traction on social media, is an example of how international solidarity can impact local movements. This campaign not only highlighted Kasha's work but also brought to light the broader struggles faced by LGBTQ individuals in Uganda.

However, the evolution of LGBTQ rights in Uganda is not without its challenges. The climate of fear and repression remains palpable, with reports of police raids on safe spaces and the harassment of LGBTQ individuals continuing unabated. Activists like Kasha often face threats to their safety, and the government has been known to use anti-LGBTQ rhetoric to distract from other pressing issues, such as corruption and economic instability.

Moreover, the rise of conservative religious movements has further complicated the fight for LGBTQ rights. These groups have gained significant influence, often framing their opposition to LGBTQ rights as a defense of traditional values. This has resulted in a backlash against any progress made, with increased hostility towards LGBTQ individuals in various spheres of life.

In conclusion, while Kasha Nabagesera's activism has catalyzed important conversations and initiatives regarding LGBTQ rights in Uganda, the journey is far from over. The evolution of LGBTQ rights since her emergence as a leader reflects a complex interplay of progress and resistance. The ongoing struggle highlights the necessity for continued advocacy, education, and international support to foster a more inclusive society. Kasha's legacy serves as both a beacon of hope and a reminder of the work that remains to be done in the pursuit of equality for all Ugandans, regardless of their sexual orientation or gender identity.

The role of LGBTQ individuals in shaping Uganda's future

The ongoing struggle for LGBTQ rights in Uganda is not just a fight for equality; it is a transformative movement that has the potential to reshape the social, political, and cultural landscape of the nation. LGBTQ individuals in Uganda are increasingly taking on roles as leaders, advocates, and change-makers, challenging the status quo and envisioning a future where diversity is celebrated rather than persecuted.

Theoretical Framework

The role of LGBTQ individuals in shaping Uganda's future can be understood through various sociological and political theories. One prominent theory is the **Social Movement Theory**, which posits that marginalized groups mobilize to advocate for their rights and interests. This framework highlights how LGBTQ activists, like Kasha Nabagesera, utilize collective identity and solidarity to challenge oppressive structures. The **Intersectionality Theory** further elucidates how LGBTQ individuals navigate multiple identities, including race, class, and gender, influencing their activism and the broader societal change.

Emergence of LGBTQ Leadership

LGBTQ individuals are increasingly emerging as leaders within their communities, fostering a sense of empowerment and resilience. Organizations such as *Freedom and Roam Uganda* (FARUG) have become platforms for LGBTQ voices, providing training and resources to help individuals develop leadership skills. This empowerment is crucial; as LGBTQ leaders gain visibility and credibility, they can influence public opinion and policy decisions.

For instance, Kasha Nabagesera's work has inspired many young activists who are now taking up the mantle. They are organizing community outreach programs, engaging in dialogue with local leaders, and advocating for legislative reforms. These efforts are essential in creating a supportive environment where LGBTQ individuals can thrive, thus fostering a culture of acceptance and inclusion.

Cultural Shifts and Visibility

Visibility plays a critical role in shaping societal attitudes towards LGBTQ individuals. As more LGBTQ individuals share their stories and experiences, they challenge stereotypes and misconceptions that fuel discrimination. Public figures, artists, and activists are utilizing various media platforms to highlight LGBTQ narratives, showcasing the rich tapestry of Ugandan society that includes diverse sexual orientations and gender identities.

An example of this cultural shift is the increasing participation of LGBTQ individuals in public events, such as pride celebrations and advocacy forums. These events not only celebrate identity but also serve as powerful statements against oppression. They provide a space for community building, fostering solidarity among LGBTQ individuals and their allies.

Political Engagement and Advocacy

The political landscape in Uganda is fraught with challenges for LGBTQ rights, particularly with the existence of discriminatory laws. However, LGBTQ individuals are increasingly engaging in political advocacy, demanding representation and policy changes. Activists are forming coalitions with human rights organizations to lobby against anti-LGBTQ legislation and promote inclusive policies.

One significant example is the coalition formed to combat the infamous "*Kill the Gays*" bill. This coalition, comprising LGBTQ activists and human rights defenders, has worked tirelessly to raise awareness both locally and internationally. Their advocacy efforts have drawn attention to the need for reform, highlighting the detrimental effects of such legislation on public health, safety, and human rights.

Education and Awareness Initiatives

Education is a powerful tool for change. LGBTQ individuals in Uganda are spearheading initiatives aimed at educating the public about sexual orientation and gender identity. Workshops, seminars, and community dialogues are being organized to dispel myths and foster understanding. These initiatives are vital in addressing the root causes of homophobia and discrimination.

For example, outreach programs targeting schools and universities are crucial in shaping the perceptions of the younger generation. By educating youth about LGBTQ issues, these programs aim to cultivate a more inclusive mindset, ultimately contributing to a future where diversity is embraced.

Building Alliances and Solidarity

The role of LGBTQ individuals in shaping Uganda's future is also marked by the building of alliances with other marginalized groups. Intersectional activism recognizes that the struggles for various rights are interconnected. LGBTQ activists are forging partnerships with women's rights organizations, disability rights groups, and other social justice movements to create a united front against oppression.

This solidarity not only amplifies the voices of LGBTQ individuals but also highlights the shared struggles faced by various marginalized communities. By working together, these groups can effectively challenge systemic inequalities and advocate for a more just society.

Conclusion: A Vision for the Future

As LGBTQ individuals continue to assert their rights and identities, they are laying the groundwork for a more inclusive Uganda. Their activism is not merely about fighting for legal recognition; it is about envisioning a future where every individual, regardless of their sexual orientation or gender identity, can live authentically and without fear.

The role of LGBTQ individuals in shaping Uganda's future is multifaceted, encompassing leadership, advocacy, education, and coalition-building. Through their resilience and determination, they are not only challenging oppressive norms but also inspiring a new generation to continue the fight for equality and justice. The journey ahead may be fraught with challenges, but the collective efforts of LGBTQ individuals are paving the way for a brighter, more inclusive future for all Ugandans.

Index

a, 1–35, 37, 38, 41–57, 59–64, 66–74, 77–81, 83–89, 93–97
ability, 13, 23, 33, 54, 63, 71, 72, 76, 77
absence, 84
abuse, 2, 7
acceptance, 3–5, 12, 16–19, 23, 24, 27, 29, 41, 42, 46, 48, 50, 54, 67, 69, 78, 79, 84, 96
access, 7, 27, 46, 79
accountability, 61
act, 3, 9, 17–19, 23, 74, 77, 94
action, 9, 26, 28, 33, 43, 54, 55, 57, 59, 61, 68, 72, 88
activism, 6, 8–12, 14–17, 19, 21, 25, 28–30, 32–38, 41–43, 45, 47, 51–55, 57, 61–63, 65, 67, 69, 71–74, 76, 77, 84–88, 91, 94, 95, 97
activist, 3, 18, 25, 26, 32, 34
adaptability, 61, 77
addition, 46, 70
adherence, 12
advancement, 85
adversity, 15, 17, 21, 27, 32, 35, 46, 54, 76, 77, 87
advice, 70

advocacy, 9, 16, 30–33, 37, 38, 42, 45, 49, 50, 52, 54–65, 67–69, 72, 76, 77, 79, 80, 83, 85–88, 92, 93, 95–97
advocate, 3, 10, 14, 17, 22, 24, 28, 33, 34, 44, 46, 54, 67, 69, 71, 72, 79, 80, 93, 94, 97
affront, 55
aftermath, 76
age, 11, 79
agenda, 61
aid, 52, 55, 79
aim, 91, 97
alertness, 74
amplification, 93
anger, 19
anticipation, 18
anxiety, 3, 8, 13, 16, 18, 20, 34, 84
approach, 33, 41–43, 46–49, 54, 59, 72, 73, 77, 79, 85
arena, 56, 61
arrest, 31, 49
aspect, 20
assault, 34
assembly, 68
assistance, 71
atmosphere, 13, 30, 44, 70, 84
attack, 51

attention, 23, 25, 33, 35, 56, 72, 86, 88
attraction, 1
audience, 48
authenticity, 17, 19
authority, 44
award, 78
awareness, 12, 14, 25, 29, 33, 46–52, 54, 55, 57, 59, 72, 80, 88, 91, 93, 94

back, 8, 76
backdrop, 1, 6, 12, 32, 67
backlash, 3, 5, 14, 16, 19–21, 24, 34, 35, 37, 42, 44, 50, 51, 57, 61, 63, 66, 73, 76, 95
balance, 14
barrier, 12, 43, 44
basis, 68
battle, 24, 32, 50, 52, 59, 80
battleground, 5
beacon, 10, 19, 22, 25, 30, 33, 45, 54, 57, 68, 71, 72, 80, 85, 87, 95
being, 13, 20, 23, 34, 66, 72, 74, 96
belief, 15, 21, 33, 79, 88
belonging, 9, 12, 13, 15, 26, 69, 79
bill, 7, 23, 32, 33, 49, 51–53, 55, 60, 80, 84, 94
blend, 1
bravery, 3, 19
bridge, 43, 45, 48
bridging, 33, 41
building, 9, 10, 22, 27, 29, 43, 49, 61, 69, 79, 80, 96, 97
bullying, 92
burden, 34

call, 77

camaraderie, 13
campaign, 60
capacity, 27, 76
case, 4, 35, 61, 62
catalyst, 17, 21, 25, 47
catharsis, 77
cause, 33, 43, 50
caution, 13, 48, 74
celebration, 27
challenge, 6, 16, 17, 24, 29, 32, 42, 44, 46–48, 67, 69, 80, 89, 96, 97
change, 8, 15, 19, 21, 24–26, 30, 33–35, 37, 42, 43, 46, 47, 49, 52, 57, 59, 67, 68, 71, 73, 77, 80, 86–89, 91, 93, 95, 96
chapter, 52
child, 11
childhood, 11, 12
choice, 19
class, 50
Claude Steele, 12
climate, 7, 31, 43, 49, 70, 77, 94
climbing, 11
coalition, 61, 68, 69, 80, 97
collaboration, 23, 37, 42, 48, 58, 59, 80, 88, 93
collection, 78
combination, 83, 93
commitment, 10, 16, 32, 33, 38, 43, 46, 49, 52, 54, 69, 81, 89, 93
community, 1, 2, 6, 8–16, 20–22, 24–30, 32–35, 41–43, 46–48, 50, 51, 53, 55–58, 61, 65–71, 79–81, 85, 87, 91, 93, 96
companion, 16

Index

compassion, 33, 42
complexity, 18, 50, 61
component, 45, 77
computer, 93
concept, 11, 12, 26, 76
concern, 29
conclusion, 17, 30, 32, 33, 46, 49, 52, 59, 61, 63, 67, 69, 73, 81, 85, 89, 93, 95
condemnation, 13, 33, 55
conflict, 5, 11, 15
confluence, 8, 30
conformity, 17
confusion, 4, 11
connection, 2, 13, 27
consequence, 86
constructivism, 47
contact, 47
content, 48
context, 1, 2, 5, 26, 47, 55, 65, 69, 76
conversation, 25
core, 22, 32, 79
cornerstone, 29, 89
corruption, 51, 94
cost, 73
counseling, 46, 79, 92
country, 1, 2, 35, 61, 71
courage, 6, 9, 14, 18, 19, 23, 25, 27, 32, 33, 35, 51, 64, 73, 88, 89
court, 68, 69
coverage, 35, 80
creativity, 27
criminalization, 67
culmination, 33
culture, 1, 13, 29, 30, 49, 96
curriculum, 79
cycle, 8, 46, 84

David Kato, 34
death, 2, 34, 51
decade, 69
decision, 3, 18, 61, 68, 80
declaration, 17, 19
decriminalization, 72
dedication, 10
defense, 95
defiance, 17, 29
demand, 25
demonstration, 77
depression, 3, 8, 16, 20, 34, 85
desire, 11, 21, 26
despair, 20
detection, 27
determination, 3, 12, 17, 22, 29, 32, 33, 50, 54, 77, 81, 88, 89, 97
detriment, 32
development, 47
deviant, 12, 47, 65
deviation, 1, 11, 15
dialogue, 18, 29, 33, 41, 43–45, 47, 48, 50, 53, 54, 68, 80, 84, 85, 88, 96
difficulty, 84
dignity, 8, 15, 42, 44, 51, 52, 57, 69
disability, 97
disappointment, 19
disbelief, 19
discourse, 45, 47, 50, 56, 62, 94
discrepancy, 61
discrimination, 6–8, 10, 12, 13, 16, 21, 23, 26, 29, 32, 42, 46, 47, 50, 57, 65, 67–69, 72, 73, 81, 83–86, 92, 94, 96, 97
dismantling, 48, 49, 79, 87
dismissal, 7

dissemination, 47, 48
dissent, 69
diversity, 6, 42, 45, 88, 95, 97
document, 52
drive, 21, 50
duality, 18
dynamic, 12, 91

East Africa, 72, 73
educate, 51
education, 2, 7, 16, 33, 42, 43, 46–49, 65, 67, 79, 81, 88, 89, 91, 94, 95, 97
effect, 14, 16, 30, 31, 33, 34, 49, 59, 64, 71, 84, 88
effectiveness, 56, 58, 61, 63, 92
emergence, 67, 69, 71, 93, 95
empathy, 24, 47–49, 66, 89
employment, 7, 16, 35, 50, 84
empowerment, 7, 13, 26, 45, 46, 48, 69, 93
encounter, 2, 6, 12, 14, 15
end, 55, 69
endeavor, 41, 52
engagement, 41, 45, 66, 68, 79, 81
entrepreneurship, 93
environment, 1, 2, 5–7, 12, 13, 15, 18, 21, 22, 24, 26, 27, 30, 34, 45, 47, 53, 54, 57, 67, 68, 70, 71, 73, 79, 94, 96
equality, 10, 15, 17, 19, 23, 30, 32, 33, 35, 38, 41, 45, 46, 51, 52, 54, 57, 59, 61, 64, 65, 67, 69, 71, 73, 78–81, 84–86, 88, 89, 92, 94, 95, 97
equation, 14–16, 22, 58, 92, 93
era, 65

establishment, 22, 27, 46, 48, 59, 79, 86
esteem, 12
estrangement, 18
event, 14, 27, 35
eviction, 84
evidence, 48, 59
evolution, 94, 95
example, 14, 25, 27–29, 33, 35, 42, 48, 50, 53, 56, 60, 71–73, 77, 96, 97
exception, 1
exchange, 55–57
existence, 14, 23, 34, 35, 96
experience, 2, 3, 8, 12, 15, 18–20, 51, 84
exploitation, 7
exposure, 13, 22, 27, 34

fabric, 6
face, 2, 7, 14, 17, 21, 24–27, 32–35, 46, 49, 50, 54, 56, 69, 70, 74, 77, 79, 84, 85, 87, 92, 94
factor, 23
failing, 20, 44, 50
faith, 24, 42–45, 53
family, 1–3, 5, 6, 11, 12, 15, 17–20, 24, 35, 46, 76
favor, 68
fear, 2, 5–8, 10, 12–14, 16, 18, 21, 26, 30, 31, 33, 34, 42, 44, 47, 49, 68, 70, 73, 74, 81, 84, 94, 97
feeling, 11–13
fervor, 55
fight, 3, 8–10, 12, 14, 15, 17, 19, 23, 27, 32, 33, 35, 37, 41, 43, 45, 46, 51, 52, 54, 57, 59,

61, 62, 65, 67–69, 72, 73, 80, 81, 85, 86, 88, 89, 92–95, 97
figure, 41, 45, 51, 59, 62
fire, 9
force, 43
forefront, 24
form, 77
formation, 5, 44
foster, 33, 49, 50, 63, 69, 71, 79, 91, 95, 97
foundation, 37, 67, 71, 89
founding, 22, 28
framework, 7, 11, 36, 69, 83, 92, 94
freedom, 68
frenzy, 94
front, 54, 55, 80, 97
fuel, 29, 41, 76, 96
funding, 22, 70, 84
future, 3, 10, 11, 30, 46, 61, 69, 73, 79–81, 85, 87–89, 95, 97

gap, 33, 41, 45, 48
gathering, 9, 12, 13
gender, 1, 6–8, 11, 12, 15, 21, 42, 46, 48, 50, 62, 66, 73, 86, 88, 91, 95–97
generation, 10, 30, 67, 73, 94, 97
globe, 33, 88
goal, 55
Gordon Allport, 47
government, 13, 33, 42, 51–54, 56, 61, 68, 69, 72, 73, 76, 80, 88, 94
grandmother, 2
groundwork, 3, 6, 93, 97
group, 9, 13, 20, 35
growth, 46, 76
guidance, 45

guise, 66

halt, 60
hand, 69
harassment, 13, 16, 34, 49, 53, 68, 69, 72–74, 84, 86, 94
hate, 7, 31, 84
head, 26, 53
health, 8, 16, 20, 48, 74, 79, 84, 85, 92, 93
healthcare, 7, 16, 50
heartbreak, 18, 74
help, 8, 85
heteronormativity, 1
heterosexuality, 15
hiding, 35, 66
highlight, 21, 27, 30, 52, 56, 62, 96
history, 79
home, 61
homophobia, 12, 17, 22, 41, 44, 51, 97
homosexual, 65
homosexuality, 6, 16, 22, 23, 31, 44, 49–51, 53, 66, 67, 72, 83, 84, 94
hope, 9, 10, 19, 22, 25, 30, 33, 43, 45, 49, 50, 54, 57, 68, 71, 72, 80, 81, 85, 87, 88, 93, 95
hostility, 1, 18, 24, 32, 50, 84, 95
housing, 35, 50
humanity, 52
hurdle, 61

idea, 61
ideal, 1
ideation, 8

identity, 1–8, 10–12, 14–17, 19–21, 24, 42, 45, 46, 48, 52, 66, 72–74, 88, 91, 95–97
ignorance, 79
immorality, 16, 66
impact, 10, 13, 18, 20, 23, 30, 34, 35, 37, 38, 43, 44, 46, 48, 61–63, 72, 73, 84, 85, 88, 89, 93
imperative, 69
import, 31
importance, 3, 6, 12, 14, 17, 19, 21, 25, 28, 32, 42, 43, 45–49, 54, 56, 59, 64, 66–68, 79, 80, 85, 86, 88
imprisonment, 13, 49, 51, 65, 67, 69, 94
impunity, 84
inclination, 11
inclusion, 43, 44, 48, 49, 84, 96
inclusivity, 33, 50, 53, 73, 88, 94
increase, 14, 48, 72
independence, 7, 65, 84
individual, 15, 18, 19, 21, 24, 33, 62, 89, 97
influence, 9, 10, 25, 59, 62, 66, 88, 94
information, 47, 48
initiative, 28, 53
injustice, 46, 77
insight, 11
inspiration, 8, 10, 33, 46, 52, 54, 80, 87
instability, 84, 94
instance, 24, 32, 34, 41, 48, 50, 53–55, 59, 66, 67, 70, 72, 76, 96
interaction, 47

interconnectedness, 55, 61, 62, 72, 73, 80, 86, 88
internalization, 12
interplay, 3, 4, 10, 11, 15, 19, 32, 37, 67, 95
interpretation, 44
intersection, 12, 27, 35, 43, 45, 52, 86
intersectionality, 50, 54, 63
intolerance, 22, 30
introduction, 13, 24, 32, 53, 94
invisibility, 31
involvement, 58
isolation, 3, 11, 12, 16, 20, 34, 35, 42, 74, 92
issuance, 68
issue, 7, 9, 29, 51, 70

John Kerry, 55
journey, 5, 6, 8–10, 12, 15–19, 21, 22, 24, 25, 32–34, 38, 43, 46, 54, 59, 65, 67, 69, 71, 85, 87, 95, 97
judgment, 12
Judith Butler's, 11
justice, 7, 8, 10, 35, 37, 47, 52, 54, 57, 61, 67, 69, 81, 84, 85, 89, 97

Kasha, 1–6, 9–25, 27–30, 32–34, 38, 41–54, 58–64, 66, 67, 72–74, 76–80, 86–89, 91–95
Kasha Nabagesera, 1, 7, 8, 15, 17, 21, 26, 31, 32, 34, 35, 37, 41, 43, 45, 47, 49–51, 59, 65, 67–69, 73, 79, 93
Kasha Nabagesera's, 3, 6, 8, 10–12, 15, 17, 19, 24, 25, 27, 30,

Index 105

    32, 33, 38, 43, 45, 46, 48,
    49, 52, 54, 57, 61, 63, 71,
    73, 81, 84, 85, 87, 89, 91,
    93, 95, 96
Kato, 34
Kenya, 72
Kimberlé Crenshaw, 62
knowledge, 46, 47, 54, 80, 86, 89

lack, 7, 8, 11, 49, 52, 71, 84, 86
landmark, 68
landscape, 3, 8, 11, 12, 15, 16, 22,
    24, 30, 32, 34, 43, 47,
    49–51, 61, 65, 67, 69, 71,
    83, 89, 91, 93, 95, 96
law, 55, 68
layer, 18, 50
leader, 63, 95
leadership, 9, 23, 46, 88, 97
legacy, 10, 30, 46, 64, 65, 73, 87, 89,
    95
legalization, 80
legislation, 24, 30–32, 49–51, 55,
    65, 70, 72, 80, 96
lens, 20, 62
level, 58
leverage, 25, 55
life, 9, 12, 14, 15, 19, 25, 26, 31, 33,
    49, 51, 65, 67, 73, 94, 95
lifeline, 2, 53, 69
lifestyle, 74
lifetime, 6
light, 56
literacy, 93
living, 3, 7, 13, 34
lobbying, 59, 61, 80
location, 14
loneliness, 74
loss, 18, 35

love, 1, 2, 18, 42, 48, 72

mainstream, 33, 41
majority, 47
manifestation, 51
mantle, 96
marginalization, 21
marriage, 80
meaning, 47, 76
means, 77, 84
media, 25, 29, 33, 35, 47, 48, 50, 61,
    66, 67, 77, 80, 83, 94, 96
meeting, 9
mentor, 45, 46, 64
mentorship, 46, 67
message, 23, 29, 48
mindset, 79, 97
minority, 47
misinformation, 22, 29, 49
mission, 21, 41
mistrust, 44
misunderstood, 12
mob, 7
mobilization, 31, 55, 68, 69
moment, 3, 12, 17, 19
momentum, 73
mother, 12, 19
movement, 12, 14, 26, 30, 34, 46, 50,
    52–55, 59, 68, 71, 78, 89,
    92, 95
murder, 34
myriad, 6, 15, 26, 32

narrative, 12, 16, 20, 25, 49, 59, 66,
    67, 71, 77, 83
nation, 95
nationalism, 61
nature, 35, 48, 69, 73
necessity, 26, 54, 68, 95

need, 8, 16, 18, 21, 25, 26, 28, 32, 33, 35, 41, 50, 61, 84, 85
neighboring, 71–73
neocolonialism, 63
network, 15, 27, 59
nonconformity, 11
notion, 25, 26, 88
number, 29

on, 9, 10, 14, 18, 22, 23, 26–28, 30, 34, 37, 42, 43, 46–54, 56–59, 61–63, 65, 68–74, 77, 80, 81, 84, 86, 88, 91–95
one, 3, 6, 12, 17, 20, 21, 27, 29, 33, 43, 46–48, 59, 67, 74, 81, 88, 89
opinion, 44
opposition, 16, 25, 50, 84, 85, 95
oppression, 8, 25, 33, 50, 54, 57, 59, 62, 65, 96, 97
order, 33
organization, 22, 23, 26
organizing, 27, 53, 69, 96
orientation, 7, 8, 13, 15, 21, 42, 43, 46, 48, 52, 62, 66, 73, 88, 91, 95–97
ostracism, 2, 6, 20, 33–35, 51, 74, 83, 85
ostracization, 23, 31
ostracizes, 45
other, 12, 29, 32, 50, 54, 59, 61, 69, 80, 85, 86, 94, 97
outcry, 32, 51, 60
outrage, 51
outreach, 22, 33, 42, 48, 96, 97
outsider, 11

pain, 9, 20, 21, 46, 76

pandemic, 71
paradox, 13
part, 9, 69
participation, 14, 96
partnership, 54
passage, 52
passion, 9, 12, 14, 17
path, 3, 6, 69
peer, 79
penalty, 51
people, 13, 42, 46, 68, 72, 89
perception, 11, 12, 24, 25, 83
performativity, 11
period, 3, 53
persecution, 6, 10, 13, 22, 24, 47, 53, 55, 59, 66, 81, 94
persistence, 32, 83
perspective, 44
place, 2, 11, 25, 73
planning, 51
platform, 25, 28, 42
play, 33, 35, 43, 66, 69
player, 23
playing, 11, 48
plight, 9, 33, 52, 55, 77
point, 9, 32
police, 68, 94
policy, 25, 42, 44, 59, 86, 96
populism, 61
portrayal, 66
position, 69
potential, 18, 22, 24, 25, 33, 37, 44, 49, 56, 59, 67, 95
poverty, 7, 51
power, 10, 15, 21, 23, 25, 33, 42, 47–49, 51, 54, 57, 59–61, 64–66, 69, 71, 73, 85–87, 94
precedent, 84

Index

prejudice, 17, 29, 47–49, 79
presence, 38
pressure, 5, 15, 24, 32, 52, 54, 55, 60, 68, 72, 80
pride, 14, 27, 35, 96
priority, 61
process, 5, 12, 17
product, 16
progress, 7, 8, 25, 32, 45, 57, 60, 66, 70, 73, 83, 85, 95
protest, 77
psychologist, 12
public, 25, 29, 35, 44, 47, 50, 51, 66, 67, 80, 87, 91, 94, 96
pursuit, 35, 54, 61, 64, 73, 95
push, 31

quality, 11
quest, 47
question, 94
quo, 6, 16, 46, 94, 95
quorum, 52, 68

race, 50, 62
rallying, 32, 51, 55, 73
reach, 29, 30, 48, 71
reaction, 8, 18, 20, 55
reality, 2
realm, 31, 72
recognition, 25, 28, 33, 43, 44, 52, 67, 71, 78, 84, 97
recourse, 84
reduction, 48
reflection, 94
reform, 79–81, 85
region, 71–73
rejection, 1, 3, 6, 16, 18, 20, 21, 24, 35, 46, 76, 85, 92
relationship, 2, 12

relief, 69
reminder, 17, 33, 64, 78, 88, 89, 95
repeal, 56
report, 48, 52, 56
representation, 11, 14, 25, 66, 67, 80, 81, 87, 96
repression, 7, 57, 63, 70, 94
reprisal, 14
resilience, 3, 9, 10, 12, 14, 17, 19, 21, 25–27, 30, 32, 33, 35, 38, 43, 46, 50, 52–54, 57, 61, 64, 65, 69–71, 76, 77, 81, 85, 87–89, 97
resistance, 11, 17, 33, 37, 44, 50, 53, 54, 59, 84, 95
resolution, 56
resolve, 10, 32
resonance, 88
resource, 50
respect, 1, 44, 80
response, 21, 29, 32, 33, 43, 55–57
responsibility, 10
result, 34, 61, 85, 87
retreat, 21
retrenchment, 61
retribution, 21
retrospect, 3
revelation, 17, 18
revival, 52
rhetoric, 31, 33, 73, 84, 94
right, 24, 68
rise, 30, 32, 61, 73, 94
risk, 20, 22, 33, 35
road, 67
role, 1, 9, 11, 23, 25, 31, 32, 35, 37, 38, 43, 45–48, 50, 52, 53, 66, 68, 69, 80, 84, 86, 94, 96, 97
room, 9, 11, 15

root, 97
ruling, 68
Rwanda, 72

s, 1–25, 27–30, 32–34, 38, 41, 43–49, 52–57, 59–64, 66–68, 71–74, 76, 77, 79–81, 84–89, 91, 93–97
sacrifice, 73
safety, 16, 22, 26, 32, 34, 35, 53, 66, 70, 74, 94
sanction, 52
scale, 61, 80
scope, 71
scripture, 44
scrutiny, 35, 51, 54, 72
search, 2
secrecy, 2, 12, 13, 26, 70
secret, 12, 13, 26, 27, 32
section, 15, 19, 23, 38, 43, 62, 87, 91
security, 79
self, 6, 11, 12, 17, 20, 46
sense, 9–16, 20, 21, 23, 25, 26, 34, 48, 69, 71, 74, 79
sentiment, 22, 43, 51
series, 30, 43, 93
set, 1, 11, 47, 84
sex, 1, 7, 13, 24, 80
sexuality, 1, 11, 15, 45, 86
shadow, 1
share, 25, 27, 32, 47, 48, 53, 54, 68, 70, 72, 92, 96
sharing, 25, 29, 47, 48, 50, 72, 88
shift, 25, 29, 44, 48, 65, 72, 87, 96
significance, 24, 25, 87
silence, 3, 19, 31, 69
sin, 84
situation, 55, 56, 84, 88
soccer, 11

socialization, 79
society, 2, 3, 5, 6, 8, 11, 12, 14–17, 19, 20, 22, 23, 25, 33, 41–46, 48–50, 53, 66, 67, 69, 73, 76, 79, 80, 85, 87–89, 91, 93, 95–97
socio, 8, 11, 16, 26, 43, 51, 83, 86
solace, 2, 13, 21
solidarity, 9, 23, 25–27, 32, 33, 35, 43, 46, 48, 50, 54, 55, 57, 59, 61–64, 69–73, 80, 81, 86, 88, 96, 97
source, 2, 20, 73
South Africa, 80
space, 2, 13, 26, 28, 53, 96
spark, 89
speaking, 33, 38, 52, 54, 66, 72, 77, 88
spectrum, 50
sphere, 67
spirit, 17, 27, 35, 71, 72, 87
stability, 7
stage, 1, 38, 57, 59, 68
stance, 54, 68, 72, 88
state, 35, 68, 74
statement, 19, 23, 55, 68
status, 6, 16, 46, 86, 94, 95
step, 14, 19, 55, 67
stereotype, 12
stigma, 6, 8, 12, 16, 22, 24, 33, 34, 42, 44, 47, 49, 50, 53, 66, 69, 70, 74, 79, 83–87
stigmatization, 6, 8
story, 17, 19, 21, 25, 33, 46, 77, 88, 89
storytelling, 48, 66, 72
strain, 34
strategy, 41, 48
strength, 2, 17, 21, 46, 76

stress, 76
struggle, 5, 12, 16, 23, 25, 27, 29, 30, 32, 37, 45, 46, 49, 50, 52, 57, 64, 69–71, 78, 80, 85, 88, 95
subsection, 17, 26, 32, 35, 47, 73
success, 29, 67
summary, 8, 10, 12, 21, 50, 54
support, 10, 14–16, 18, 20–25, 27–30, 33, 35–37, 45, 46, 50–54, 59, 61, 63, 67, 69–72, 79, 80, 84–86, 88, 92, 93, 95
surge, 9
surveillance, 57
survey, 48
suspension, 7, 32
sustainability, 70
symphony, 59
system, 46

tailoring, 93
tale, 87
Tanzania, 72, 73
tapestry, 96
target, 63
task, 2, 22, 44
team, 22
technicality, 49, 52, 84, 94
tenacity, 54
term, 62, 91
terrain, 16
testament, 6, 10, 19, 21, 27, 33, 35, 38, 54, 71, 73, 86, 87
theme, 21
theory, 20, 26, 35, 47, 55, 68, 69, 76
threat, 8, 12, 13, 20, 22, 27, 34, 49–52, 70, 84, 85
time, 13, 32, 54, 55, 71

toll, 3, 5, 13, 34, 73, 74, 84, 92
tool, 25, 42, 66, 79, 96
town, 1
traction, 59
trade, 55
training, 48, 93
transfer, 46
transformation, 47, 49, 69
transition, 12
trauma, 2, 34, 76
trend, 55
triumph, 87
truth, 18, 52
turmoil, 17
turning, 9

U.S., 55, 61
Uganda, 1–4, 6–17, 19–30, 32–35, 37, 38, 41, 43, 45–47, 49–57, 59, 61, 64–74, 77–81, 83–85, 87–89, 91–97
Uganda, 55
Ugandan, 11, 22, 25, 33, 42, 49, 52, 53, 57, 68, 91
uncertainty, 13, 84
underpinning, 43, 47
underreporting, 31
understanding, 2, 8, 12, 13, 15, 24, 25, 29, 33, 41–43, 45, 47–51, 53, 54, 62, 66, 67, 79, 83, 84, 88, 97
unity, 43, 59
universality, 72
university, 13
upbringing, 1
urgency, 23
use, 25, 94

victory, 52, 68
view, 6, 83
violence, 2, 6–8, 13, 16, 21–23, 26, 29, 31, 33–35, 42, 47, 49, 51, 53, 57, 63, 67–69, 73, 74, 83–86, 94
visa, 61
visibility, 3, 14, 22–25, 27, 30, 54, 63, 87
vision, 21, 79–81, 88
voice, 3, 42, 78
vulnerability, 33, 71, 84, 85
Vygotsky, 47

wave, 55, 62, 71
way, 43, 45, 67, 97

web, 85
whole, 25
wildfire, 20
will, 25, 30, 46, 58, 61, 69, 79, 80, 89
willingness, 48, 69
win, 68
woman, 18
work, 1, 10, 12, 25, 30, 38, 43, 48, 49, 59, 61–63, 71, 73, 85–88, 93, 95, 96
workforce, 93
world, 2, 12, 13, 30, 55, 63, 68, 89

youth, 45, 46, 48, 67, 88, 92, 94, 97
Yoweri Museveni, 51